For Lucy, Tom and Sarah

CONTENTS

STEP OUT OF YOUR
FRONT DOOR
30

INTRODUCTION   12

THE 'ONE DAY'
ADVENTURE
18

A 5-TO-9
ADVENTURE
32

UNDER A
HARVEST MOON
22

A COMMUTER'S
ADVENTURE
36

WALKING HOME
FOR CHRISTMAS
25

A JOURNEY AROUND
YOUR HOME
40

USE YOUR
WEEKEND
28

CATCH IT,
COOK IT, EAT IT
45

ENTER A RACE 48

A CREDIT CARD ADVENTURE 70

AN OUT OF OFFICE EXPERIENCE 52

WOODS AND FORESTS 77

A GLASGOW NIGHT OUT 54

RIVER SWIM 80

COAST TO COAST – AN ANCIENT JOURNEY 59

ROMAN ROAMIN' 84

COAST TO COAST – A WILD JOURNEY 66

SEA ADVENTURE 88

BACK TO BASICS
97

CANAL JOURNEY
111

CLOSE YOUR EYES. GO!
100

AN IMPROMPTU ESCAPE FROM THE OFFICE
114

ISLAND CAMP
104

WILDERNESS ADVENTURE
118

FAMILY TREE
106

BUILDING A WILD HUT
124

A JOURNEY FROM SOURCE TO SEA
108

A JOURNEY ON THE TUBE
127

GOING OUT
FOR DINNER
133

A RAFTING
ADVENTURE
153

SOLSTICE
ADVENTURE
137

A MOUNTAIN
ADVENTURE
157

FROM SUMMIT
TO SEA
139

A JOURNEY TO THE
END OF MY COUNTRY
167

THE BIVVY
CHALLENGE
144

AN M25
ADVENTURE
176

A CIRCULAR
JOURNEY
146

HOW TO HAVE YOUR OWN
MICROADVENTURE   182

INDEX   250
ACKNOWLEDGEMENTS   256

'Adventure is a state of mind,
a spirit of trying something new
and leaving your comfort zone.
It's about enthusiasm, ambition,
open-mindedness and curiosity.'

INTRODUCTION

Half a lifetime ago, I left home to spend a year in Africa. That was it. I was hooked. Adventure! Since then I have spent years on the open road, chasing the spirit of adventure across the planet. I've visited almost half the countries on Earth and still itch to explore all those that remain undiscovered to me. I have rowed and sailed across oceans, walked across deserts and cycled across continents. I do it because it is fun. I do it because it is miserable and difficult but also because it is easier in many ways than the complicated confusion and stress and hassle of modern life. I do it because I love the wild, silent beauty of the empty places on our planet. And I do it because I love the teeming, vibrant fullness of our planet and the surprising, memorable interactions with the random selection of seven billion souls I bump into along the way.

My adventures have taught me so much about the world and about myself. They have given me more focus, purpose and perspective than I used to have. I have spent the last decade or so writing books and blogs and giving talks about my adventures. I am very fortunate that my passion and hobby has become my job. I've spent years paying my bills and taxes (did I mention the stress and hassle of modern life?) through my adventures.

So I felt a fair degree of hesitation when I decided to dedicate a year to exploring my own not-very-wild country. I was not going to embark on the sort of big, exciting adventures that are the traditional fare of career adventurers. I was going small. Really small. Tiny adventures. Smaller even that that, perhaps – I was going in search of *micro*adventures close to home.

What made me decide to do this? I am aware that most people do not have the time or the money to live as adventurously as they might like. But

these need not be limiting factors. And the benefits and enjoyment I derive from adventure felt too important to me to not try to share with as many people as possible.

Over time a couple of things have become clear to me, through emails on my blog and chatting to people at talks I give. Firstly, almost everyone loves vicarious adventure. The terrifying ranks of the North Yorkshire Women's Institute enjoy hearing about far-off lands and the call of the wild just as much as a Gore-Tex-clad audience at the Kendal Mountain Film Festival or Royal

The second thing I learned was that giving talks, having a website and printing cheap business cards describing myself as an 'Adventurer' somehow set me apart from the people who heard me speak or stumbled across my blog. Time after time I heard variations of this refrain: 'You are an Adventurer. I am a Normal Person.'

That is total rubbish. I am an Adventurer, but I am also a Normal Person. The only difference between me and other people is that I've managed to cobble together the time, the money, the kit and the fitness necessary to do various big expeditions. I am not stronger or more heroic than Normal People. Absolutely not.

Most people enjoy adventure and would love to have more of it in their lives, but most people don't have the time to cycle round the world. But adventure should not only be for 'Adventurers'. So I realised that what I wanted to do was to break down the barriers to adventure. And thus the microadventure was born.

I will define what I feel a microadventure is shortly but, first of all, I should define adventure. It's important to do it this way round because it is vital not to consider a microadventure as a diluted, inferior version of an adventure. It is not. A microadventure is an adventure.

Adventure is a loose word that means different things to different people. It is a state of mind, a spirit of trying something new and leaving your comfort zone. Adventure is about enthusiasm, ambition, open-mindedness and curiosity.

If this is true, then 'adventure' is not only crossing deserts and climbing mountains; adventure can be found everywhere, every day, and it is up to us to seek it out.

You probably can't go on huge adventures all the time (we all have to pragmatically juggle the commitments and constraints of our 'real lives'), but you can have a microadventure. Because you do not need to fly to the other side of the planet to find wilderness and beauty. Adventure is stretching yourself, mentally, physically or culturally. It is about doing something you do not normally do, pushing yourself hard and doing it to the best of your ability. You do not need to be an elite athlete, expertly trained, or rich to have an adventure.

So a microadventure is an adventure that is close to home: cheap, simple, short, and yet very effective. It still captures the essence of big adventures, the challenge, the fun, the escapism, the learning experiences and the excitement. All these things remain.

A microadventure has the spirit (and therefore the benefits) of a big adventure; it's just all condensed into a weekend away, or even a midweek escape from the office. Even people living in big cities are not very far away from small pockets of wilderness.

Adventure is all around us, at all times, even during hard financial times such as these; times when getting out into the wild is more invigorating and important than ever.

'So a microadventure is an adventure that is close to home: cheap, simple, short, and yet very effective. It still captures the essence of big adventures, the challenge, the fun, the escapism, the learning experiences and the excitement.'

This is a book about adventure: adventure that is accessible to everyone. There are adventures in this book that you can attempt even if you are really busy or have never climbed a mountain. There are adventures in wild places that you can tackle whether you are a young child or a disabled adult.

Maybe you live in a big city or feel that Britain is boring and crowded, or that adventure exists only in the Yukon or Patagonia. Perhaps you enjoyed camping as a child but have now grown up, got

THE 'ONE DAY' ADVENTURE

'One day I'd like to do a big adventure.' I hear this all the time: at parties, at events I speak at, by email from strangers. 'But I don't have the time / money / fitness / shiny kit.'

Time Required:	One day
Difficulty Level:	Easy
Location:	Wherever you live
Essential Extra Kit:	Map, compass

The excuses vary occasionally, but the essence remains the same: 'One day I want adventure in my life, but, unfortunately, it can't be right now'.

Waiting for all your stars to align is a guaranteed way to ensure that the adventure you crave will never happen. Waiting until you somehow, suddenly and simultaneously, have both loads of money *and* plenty of time is daft (if you'll excuse me being a bit direct before we have got to know one another properly).

One day? What rubbish!

If this applies to you, listen! You do not need a winning lottery ticket to have an adventure. What you need is a polite kick up the backside! A push. I want this book to give you the tiny bit of momentum needed to get started. This is a book for people who want adventure in their life but find that real life has got in the way.

'One day' is just an excuse. It's lazy, self-deluding and – worst of all – completely unnecessary. So if you are procrastinating and dithering about committing to adventure, why don't you begin with a one day adventure, something so tiny that it can barely be called

② UNDER A HARVEST MOON

If you want to start incorporating microadventures into your life, the most important thing to do is change your perspective. Begin seeking out wildness and adventure close to home, in seemingly familiar and humdrum places. The more you look, the more you will find. One way to help this mind shift is by going somewhere you know very well, but at night.

Time Required:	One evening
Difficulty Level:	Easy
Location:	Your house
Essential Extra Kit:	Torch, spare batteries, tripod for your camera

The world becomes a very different place after dark, and even the most gentle of landscapes can feel like a place where the wild things are.

Different senses come to the fore, and your imagination can run wild.

A full moon casts enough light to walk by and 'when the soft silver drips shimmering' it is a beautiful time to explore. It is sad how much we tend to lose touch with the natural world, particularly if we live in towns and never experience proper darkness. This is why I appreciate dates like the solstices, the equinoxes and the monthly full moon, which prod me to pay more attention to the ebb and flow of the seasons happening out there, out beyond the tepid glow of the TV screen and the orange street lamps.

I set out one evening to explore close to my home by the light of the harvest moon. The harvest moon is the full moon that appears closest to the autumn equinox in September. It is my second-favourite full moon. Yes, I really did just write that sentence. My favourite full moon is a supermoon (see page 91), which appears to be extra large as it is closer to the earth than all other full moons. (I love a blue moon, too, but they're pretty rare. They only appear once in a, once in a... I'm lost for a suitable idiom...)

All full moons rise around sunset, but only at harvest time does this continue for several days afterwards. Normally the moon is only helpful to evening hikers in the days leading up to the full moon, for in the days afterwards it rises too late to be useful. The reasons for this require too much intellect for this book to explain. Suffice to say this: it's nice to be out on the nights around the harvest full moon. You'll be able to watch the moon rise. It is eye-catching and impressive when it is close to the horizon.

You don't need to be ambitious when heading out after dark. In fact, the simpler you keep the plan, the more likely you are to actually do it. I settled on an extremely easy plan. I would follow a railway line out of town and use it to guide me as I weaved my way across the countryside, and then I'd catch a late train home from a village station when I'd had enough.

I wanted to begin in a town to experience just how different the open countryside feels at night – street lights suck the night and all its raw beauty from the world. But even in the town I felt myself paying more attention to the world than I do during the day. I was walking east, in the direction of the rising moon; I could see its glow on the horizon, silhouetting the rooftops and chimneys as it crept up into the sky.

Other senses come to the fore after dark. I felt the warmth radiating from the engine of a recently parked car. A man passed, walking a dog, and I caught the scent of his shampoo. I turned onto a quiet and deserted residential street, on which I heard the low hum of the distant motorway. A train rushed past. I stopped to listen to its receding sound and then followed along in its wake.

I was taking photographs as I went. This dramatically slowed my progress. Photography at night takes a long time because you have to use a tripod and a long exposure. Whenever I decided to take a picture I had to frame it, manually focus and then stand around for 30 seconds waiting for the exposure to finish. But I enjoyed the way this forced me to be still and observe the world around me more carefully.

A woman outside a pub stood and watched me framing a shot. I didn't notice her until she called out, quietly, 'happy photography!' She had left her friends inside, stepped out for a cigarette, and was enjoying the moon like me. I smiled back, 'happy smoking!'

The darkness at the edge of town was distinct. The houses and the street lights ended and in front of me was the abrupt blackness of an empty field. It didn't feel too much of a stretch to describe it as 'the wild'. Clouds drifted swiftly across the fat round moon, by now about a hand's breadth above the horizon. A hand's breadth meant I'd been walking for an hour since moonrise (see page 228 for an explanation of this).

I stepped into the field, crossing the boundary into a different world. I didn't use a torch; the point of this walk was to enjoy the moonlight and embrace the differences and the uncertainties of the night. I didn't want to artificially beam a thin shaft of weak light across my adventure. It took some moments to adjust to the darkness and the stillness, but as I walked along the margins of the ploughed field my eyes began to adjust. Planes circled in the sky, sweeping slowly across the constellations. The sky was much lighter than the land, and the trees at the edge of my field jutted, black, up into the rusty suburban sky. If I stood still and stared at the moon for long enough I could actually see it moving,

creeping higher across the sky. I heard insects chirping in the verges and I caught a glimpse of a rabbit sprinting by. But what surprised me was that I also *heard* the rabbit's rapid footsteps. I have never heard a rabbit before.

Field after field I enjoyed the darkness more and more. I felt adrift on a dark sea of tranquillity. It was a perfect antidote to my desk-bound day, rinsing through the tangled irritations in my mind. The evening was warm and breezy and I relished strolling down the footpaths through the fields, crossing occasional roads and walking, unseen, past homes and farms.

I had earmarked a railway station about 20 miles away from which I would catch the last train home, but I had been moving so slowly that I was never going to get that far before it departed. So when I reached the next station I decided to call it a night and head home. I was amazed at how quick the return train journey was – I had walked such a tiny distance. But it had been an extremely relaxing, enlightening way of getting a new perspective on a landscape whose blandness and over-familiarity often bores me. I promised myself that I would repeat this full moon experience more often.

OTHER IDEAS LIKE THIS

This microadventure is about looking at familiar places in a fresh way. You could, for example, cycle a different route to work or devise a 'Big Five safari challenge' in your own town. In London that might be something like this:

- **Mammal:** Spot a deer in Greenwich or Richmond Park (or perhaps a Blue Whale in the Natural History Museum?)
- **Bird:** Look up for a peregrine falcon in Battersea, parakeets in Peckham, or perhaps the ostrich in London Zoo?
- **Tree:** The Berkeley Plane is known as 'Britain's most expensive tree'.
- **Butterfly:** Keep on red alert for a Red Admiral. Try and spot a Large Blue butterfly too. Hint for identification: it's blue, and large... (Not really, it's actually pretty tiny and very rare.)
- **Reptile:** There are poisonous snakes even in London: head for Hounslow Heath for a chance to spot an adder.

WALKING HOME
FOR CHRISTMAS

It was the week before Christmas, and although the land, the roads were busy with people on their way to spend time with their families

Time Required:	Up to you
Difficulty Level:	Medium
Location:	From your home to wherever you will spend Christmas
Essential Extra Kit:	Mince pies, Santa hat, Christmas jumper, head torch

It's a lovely time of year for most, and one in which the nation is at its most cheerful and friendly. So instead of pushing my warm glow of festive goodwill to breaking point by sitting in a massive traffic jam, I decided to walk home for Christmas.

I was going to spend Christmas in Kent. I lived in a flat in London. The journey to Kent was one I made regularly. It was neither a long nor scenic journey, but I hoped that walking the route, rather than driving or taking the train as I normally did, would turn it into an interesting little challenge. The additional bonus would be arriving with some new memories and a suitably Christmas-sized appetite.

Instead of ducking my warm
glow of festive goodwill to
breaking point by sitting in a
massive traffic jam, I decided
to walk home for Christmas.

I didn't want to trudge through the miles without
paying attention to where I was – this walk wasn't
just about getting to the end. So I challenged
myself to tell the story of the walk as I went.

I would use my phone to post regular snippets on
Twitter as I walked. I didn't know whether anyone
else would be interested in following my progress
across east London, but it certainly added to my
own experience of the adventure.

Heading out my front door. I'm walking home
  for Xmas.
The first grey of dawn. Walking past MI6 at
  Vauxhall.
Commuters whizz past on bikes. Hmm…
  Perhaps I should have ridden?

Big Ben peals 8am. London's streets are quiet this morning.

Trumpet rendition of 'O Come, All Ye Faithful' drifts across the Thames.

Less than 2hrs have gone by and I stop for coffee. I am neither as tough nor as tight as I used to be!

At Tower Bridge now. Ticking off the icons.

Grey sky, grey earth: east London is depressing today.

Reached Canary Wharf, the former hub of smug.

Not much Xmas cheer in Lewisham...

...stare at the geezers to show them you're not lightweight.

A woman drags a dog down the street as it tries to crap.

Into the eastern hemisphere at Greenwich.

Eating a mince pie and walking through Greenwich Park. Trees and green spaces are good for the soul on this walk.

On Blackheath Common where the London Marathon begins. Used to be v dangerous – highwaymen!

Is there a McD's on the A207 east of Blackheath?! Hungry...

On the 'Green Chain Walk' now. A blessing to be off-road.

'It was neither a long nor epic journey, but I hoped that walking the route ... would turn it into an interesting little challenge.'

A long haul up Shooters Hill. Hoping it's all downhill from here.

Big long downhill – my kingdom for a bicycle!

5hrs' walk from my flat I see the first sheep and field. Goodbye London!

Walking down an old Roman road on my way home for Xmas.

Food! I'm lovin' it!

Just waved at 2 grannies. Big grins. Think they fancy me...

Passed a pub that's having a 'meat raffle' tonight.

Approaching Dartford. Light seeping from an already pallid day. Only about 2 more hours to go.

Firemen collecting cash for a kids' charity. First festive thing I've seen since leaving London.

I wish I had counted all the fast-food joints on this walk. No wonder the UK is fat.

7.5 hrs' walk from London and I cross the jammed M25.

Bluewater, a Mecca of seasonal materialism.

Made it! 9.5 hrs' walk from London to Kent. Time to relax now!

OTHER IDEAS LIKE THIS

Run home from a party. When I was training for a marathon I used to run home from all my evenings out. I loved running through the streets of London after a night out or dinner at a friend's house. At times I was a little too full or tipsy for optimum athletic endeavour, but I always enjoyed the adventure of seeing my city in a different way and discovering new parts of it.

Visit your parents' birthplaces (pages 106–7).

Take a journey around your home (pages 40–3).

Shake up your commute (pages 36–9).

Cycle all the streets from the Monopoly board or from the first street to the last street in your town's A–Z.

USE YOUR WEEKEND

Time Required:	One weekend
Difficulty Level:	Up to you
Location:	Within a few hours' of your house
Essential Extra Kit:	Friends
Find Out More:	Watch the Video

If you add up all your weekends, statutory leave and Bank Holidays, you'll discover you have about 130 free days each year. And that's without the occasional 'sick' day on sunny days or Test Match days. That's a long time. You could row across the Indian Ocean in 130 days, or cycle to Africa. The trouble, of course, is the fragmented nature of these 130 days, so the adventurous soul with a proper job has to be determined to make the most of their weekends rather than frittering them away at IKEA or watching *The X Factor*.

Annoyingly, I live about as far from proper wilderness as is possible in Britain. And yet by lunchtime on Saturday I can still be high on a Welsh hillside, breathing in fresh air, looking down over the sunlit Bristol Channel, and about to scare myself silly on a downhill mountain bike trail.

Here is the secret: get up early. Get up early and you'll have time to get up high. Not stupid early, if you can't bear that, but for every sacrificed hour of sleep you receive, in exchange, one glorious hour somewhere beautiful. It's a fair swap. So, rise early. Embrace the darkness. Eat breakfast. Don't faff. And go.

Before lamenting a weekend as being too short and the hills too far away, bear in mind this tale. In the 1980s a mountaineering club in London mastered the art of filling their weekends. Leaving

work at 5pm on Friday they would drive through the night to Scotland, arriving in the Highlands by dawn. They would climb mountains right through the weekend, then drive back overnight on Sunday in time for work – a round trip of 1,300 miles. You can do a lot in a weekend.

There were three of us; we had been friends since school. The bikes were on the roof. The car was filled with childish laughter and old jokes. We left London, dashed down the M4, and by late morning we were cycling up a muddy track in the Afan Forest Park. It felt a million miles away from London. We got wet and muddy, hungry and cold. We cycled and laughed all afternoon. It was brilliant.

'For every sacrificed hour of sleep you receive, in exchange, one glorious hour somewhere beautiful. It's a fair swap. So, rise early. Embrace the darkness. Eat breakfast. Don't faff. And go.'

And that's about it. There's not much more to say. It certainly wasn't very tough or impressive (all three of us wimped out of the scariest runs), and we weren't even camping. But that wasn't the point of this weekend. It was a weekend about breaking boring routines, trying something new, going somewhere different and getting out of a rut.

So if you think camping would be a barrier to doing that, then skip that bit. Stay in a B&B. Go to a pub. Do whatever you need to do just to kick-start new ideas and begin new habits.

Don't make the mistake of thinking that because you only have the weekends free you can't do anything different or interesting or adventurous. Use whatever time you have available, whatever gear and money and skills you have, to squeeze in something new. The big adventures can come later. Start small – and start this weekend. Make stuff happen.

OTHER IDEAS LIKE THIS

- There are many different ways of enjoying the countryside by bike. The purpose-built trails at a mountain bike trail centre are a good way to test yourself and improve your skills. Search online for a local one. Some excellent trails are at Coed y Brenin, Glentress, Cannock Chase and Dalby Forest.
- Coasteering is an exciting, challenging and fun way of exploring the rocky coastline of Britain. Search online for a company certified by the British Coasteering Federation to go with.
- Enter a weekend team challenge event for charity such as the Trailwalker.
- Find a taster weekend course in something you've never done before. Search online and you can find all sorts of weekends away, from climbing, kayaking or sailing, to photography, bird watching or mushroom foraging. These make excellent presents too.
- Ride the Tour de Yorkshire (pages 70–5).
- Explore the Isle of Wight (pages 146–51).
- Once you get into the habit of cramming your weekends full of adventure you can begin to get more audacious: Mont Blanc in a weekend, anyone?

STEP OUT OF YOUR FRONT DOOR

⑤

I was busy. Too busy to head off on adventures. (The irony of being too busy writing a book about microadventures to be able to go on a microadventure was not lost on me.)

Time Required:	One night's sleep
Difficulty Level:	Easy
Location:	Your garden
Means of Transport:	None
Essential Extra Kit:	Duvet and pillow

The hours and days behind the computer had begun to mount up and blur forgettably together. Meanwhile, outside, spring was galloping towards summer. The weather had been terrible. The world was drab and mute beneath a damp grey blanket of cloud. It had been like this for as long as I could remember.

But at times like these, if you look – really look – you can always notice things that are changing out there. The swallows were returning from Africa. The trees were slowly but inexorably filling with leaves. Everything was anticipating summer. I should have been doing the same…

Yesterday evening was calm and dry. I noticed this only because I noticed the absence of rain and wind. I had worked at my desk until the day was gone and the sky was dark against my window. I stopped only because it was time to sleep. In the morning I would return to my computer and write all day again. I got ready for bed (pyjamas, teddy, bed pan…). I did this every day. But suddenly I decided to do something different, to escape, if only briefly, from my boring hamster wheel.

So I fetched my sleeping bag and a head torch, grabbed a pillow and a book, and walked into the garden to sleep outside. I felt a little silly, climbing into an expedition-quality sleeping bag then lying down on my lawn. I spend a lot of nights in that bag, but not usually with a soft pillow in a garden. You could use your duvet if you prefer.

Yet the novelty alone was refreshing and amusing. I tried to read my book but the night was full of distractions. It was noisier than I expected, even without hearing a nightingale or an owl. A gentle breeze rustled through the tree above me. I counted stars and satellites. I savoured knowing that if it rained I could just scamper indoors to my bed rather than enduring a wet night.

I woke as the sun rose and grinned as I realised that I had slept in my garden. I hadn't done that since I was a little boy. I felt more relaxed and cheerful than I normally do first thing in the morning, so I lay for a few minutes just absorbing the sights and sounds of springtime. Then, grateful for sunlight on the garden, I stood up, bundled my things in my arms, and walked inside for breakfast.

OTHER IDEAS LIKE THIS

- ➔ One weekend morning, have your breakfast outdoors. Take a camping stove to the woods or park and enjoy bacon sandwiches and a cup of al fresco coffee.
- ➔ Eat your dinner in the garden, even on a cold winter night. Wrap up warm and enjoy the experience for how different it is.
- ➔ Instead of your usual morning run followed by a shower, try running to your local river for an early morning swim.
- ➔ Exercise in the park instead of the gym: mixing press-ups, burpees and the 'plank' with fartlekking or hill reps is a fantastic workout. Download the audio track for the dreaded 'beep test' onto your MP3 player for a short, painful outdoor workout that will look very strange to onlookers.
- ➔ If, like me, you live in a part of the UK blighted with night-time light pollution (in other words, a town or a city), then head for a Dark Sky area to reacquaint yourself with how impressive a dark sky filled with stars is. Search online for Dark Sky maps and organisations.
- ➔ If you've got a hammock and know how to tie yourself safely to a tree, then sleeping up a tree is a lot of fun.

A 5-TO-9
ADVENTURE

Time Required:	16 hours
Best Time to Do It:	Weekdays
Difficulty Level:	Medium
Location:	A nearby hill
Essential Extra Kit:	Bivvy bag, toothbrush
Find Out More:	Watch the Video

Many adventurous alter egos are restricted by 9-to-5 jobs. But what about the 5-to-9? What about those 16 glorious hours of freedom between leaving work in the evening and returning the next day?

It's interesting to imagine our usual 24 hours from a different perspective. We tend to perceive the main part of our day to be the 9-to-5 and then just pad out the other waking hours. But how about, just once, flipping this idea on its head? Get the 9-to-5 out of the way and then cram the rest with as much activity as possible. This book is about making the most of all your free time. I know life is more complicated than this – that you may work longer hours, have evening commitments and so on – but please at least consider it theoretically.

What adventure could you squeeze in between 5pm and 9am, if only just once? Leave a plate of food for the cat, kids and other half and head for the hills!*

I packed a rucksack (see pages 198–202 for a kit list) then jumped on a train at 5pm, bound for the nearest area of hilly countryside. We think nothing about taking a train for a day trip somewhere, so why not use it for a night away? Tell somebody where you are going and when you'll be back – and then go!

As the train gathered speed, I unfolded my map and made a plan. The train journey took about an hour and a half so I had plenty of time to scout out a good spot in which to spend the night. (Over time I have become very blasé about sleeping in the countryside. For your first attempts you might find pages 190–1 helpful for hatching plans of your own. A bit of advance planning will help decrease the anxiety you might feel about heading into the unknown until it becomes second nature.)

'I looked up at the crescent moon. It was a dark night and the stars were bright. I felt very alone, but in a liberating way.'

Arriving in the countryside, I changed into comfy clothes, shoved my suit into my rucksack and began walking up the nearest hill. It was dark already but I didn't mind. Climbing hills in the dark is fun; you become more sensitive to the sounds and smells of the evening, and it feels more exciting. It was a mild spring evening and my back was chilled with sweat by the time I removed my rucksack on the breezy summit.

I unrolled my sleeping bag and bivvy bag on a soft patch of grass. Far below, small clusters of village lights scattered across the blackness. I had slipped the surly bonds of Earth and left all the boring stuff behind. Down there was a different world. It was nice to have to wait for morning before I could enjoy the summit view. I liked the anticipation.

I looked up at the thin crescent moon. It was a dark night and the stars were bright. I felt very alone, but in a liberating way rather than a lonely way. It was half past nine. I snuggled down into my sleeping bag and fell asleep. Not only was I on an adventure, I would actually get more sleep than on a normal night back home.

I was woken by the rising sun. I poked my head out of the sleeping bag, sat up and looked around. A big smile spread across my face, something that rarely happens when I have just woken up. I smiled because the view that greeted me was more interesting than my bedroom. And I smiled because I had just slept on top of a hill.

This was an undeniably silly thing to do, but the world was wrapped in a beautiful, pale misty light. I could smell the freshness of the day. And I had this all to myself. The lonely cool dawn is the 'Wow' moment, if you have not already experienced it, when you feel vindicated in your decision to sleep on a hilltop. To wake early but refreshed on top of the world, with a view more uninterrupted than from any five-star hotel.

I know that microadventures are no panacea, no solution to genuine problems and unhappiness, but, at moments like this, they really do have power. Waking on a hilltop, even a small hill, on a sunny morning cannot fail to help put things in perspective and to infuse a sense of well-being, if only for a short while.

And 'only for a short while' is the point of this particular microadventure – because you still need to be at work on time! So I packed away my sleeping bag and began jogging down the hill. I enjoyed feeling my legs warm up as I bounced down the grassy hill. I was running to warm up and because I enjoy running, but also because I had a train to catch. There was just enough time for a quick swim in the still waters of a small lake (freezing but glorious) followed by a warming cup of tea and a bacon butty (glorious *and* hot) at the station cafe.

Commuter trains have a knack of crushing feelings of well-being. But as I type this, in an over-hot, over-expensive, over-crowded carriage on my way home, I know that the memory of waking alone in the silver-hazed silence of sunrise and plunging into that lake will stay with me for a long time.

'Waking on a hilltop on a sunny morning cannot fail to help put things into perspective and to infuse a sense of well-being, if only for a short while.'

The first time I ever spent a night like this was on the Pentland Hills outside Edinburgh when I was a student. Buffeted by winter wind while the warm lights of the city twinkled in the distance, this was where I first learned of the joys of sleeping out without a tent. I have enjoyed it ever since.

Sleeping on a hilltop is a cheap and straightforward microadventure. I can't think of many easier ways of getting a quick fix of re-focusing, re-prioritising and contentment. It seems that a sleeping bag and a Scotch egg on top of a hill are all I need to make me happy…

Strolling into work you might look a bit crumpled, especially if you used your bundled-up suit as a hilltop pillow, but it's a small price to pay. Just make sure to nonchalantly ask your colleagues if they did anything interesting last night…

*I don't really advocate leaving your kids at home to dine on cat food for the night. Take them with you. They'll love it!

OTHER HILLS TO TRY

Make sure you are properly equipped for these mountains as British weather can change very quickly. But some famously pretty peaks that would be great to sleep on include:

- Suilven, in Inverpolly, Scotland.
- Liatach, in Torridon, Scotland.
- Ben More, Scotland – the most northerly Munro, glorious and isolated in the heart of the Flow Country, Europe's largest blanket bog.
- Tryfan, in Conwy, Wales.
- Cadair Idris (there's a lovely lake for a swim there too), Gwynedd, Wales.
- Ditchling Beacon, in East Sussex, England.
- Worcestershire Beacon, in the Malvern Hills, England.

But the very best hill is the one close to where you live. That makes it more likely that you will actually go and climb it. If you have difficulty climbing a hill then sleep in a field, a cave, a snow hole, a cemetery, or even your garden (see page 30). Just do something to squeeze an adventure into your '5-to-9'. If you feel that you live too far from beautiful landscapes to be able to try this idea, then I hope that the microadventures in this book will persuade you otherwise: many take place within an hour of a city.

I believe that this chapter is the most important in the whole book. It really captures the essence of the microadventure. I'd love you to try it. Go on! If you hate it, get in touch (@al_humphreys / #microadventure) and tell me that I'm an idiot. You will return to your home and your bed more appreciative of the small things in life than you were previously. And, if you learn that you actually are happiest just staying at home, then congratulations! That's a nice thing to realise.

TIPS FOR KEEPING ON TIME

If you do try this trip, here are a few thoughts on timings to help it run more smoothly.

- ➔ Type the word 'sunset' into Google. It will tell you instantly the time of tonight's sunset at your location. This will help you get your head round how much of this microadventure will take place in the dark. It's not good or bad either way, but it is helpful to know.
- ➔ Similarly, Googling 'sunrise' will tell you when the sun rises. It gets light about half an hour before that time. Assuming you need to be back at work for 9am, you are probably going to be more governed by your office hours than sunrise.
- ➔ How much you faff in the evening doesn't matter, you will still get plenty of sleep. But in the morning you have a train to catch. On paper, all you need to do is stuff a sleeping bag into a rucksack, put your shoes on, and get going. But I am always amazed how long it takes first-timers to do this.
- ➔ So the safest way to make sure you catch your train in the morning is to set the alarm for the earliest hour you can bear. If it is summer it will be light anyway and it is nice to have a bit of time to savour the experience.
- ➔ If you need to catch a train, don't try to cook breakfast or even prepare a hot drink in the morning. It's another thing that always takes longer than you imagine. Worry about breakfast once you are off the hill.

⑦ A COMMUTER'S ADVENTURE

Time Required:	One evening after work
Difficulty Level:	Low
Location:	Your commute
Essential Extra Kit:	Briefcase, deodorant
Find Out More:	Watch the Video

Every day, millions of people commute to work. For most this is a tedious, expensive, time-wasting part of the day. But a commute can offer an easy opportunity for an occasional microadventure during a spell of nice weather, or if your daily journey is beginning to get you down.

You probably take the same route to work every day, but how much do you really know about this journey? How much do you see? Next time you are on the train, look up for a few minutes from your phone or newspaper and look out of the window at the world. As you race through towns and villages you can miss the places in between: the fields and woods and pockets of countryside that sit amongst even the most built-up regions. It is easy not to notice them. Look beyond the grey suits and sleepy eyes and free tabloid newspapers. What is it like out there? How would it feel to sit on that small hilltop and watch the trains rattling past? Where does that footpath beside the stream lead? What can you hear in that copse of trees when the sun sets and the birds settle down to roost? There's a pertinent quote from *Swallows and Amazons* that describes 'one of those places seen from the train that belong to a life in which we shall never take part'.

One evening, when you finish work, why not walk or cycle or run the route of your commute? You could go all the way home, but even better would be to pick out a peaceful spot along the way and spend the night there. A night in the wild beyond the fringes of the city you work in. A blast of wildness sandwiched between two days in the office. Make it happen. Find out for yourself how it feels to sleep in that small copse and discover what the world is like out there.

The next morning, simply get back onto the train at the closest station – usual time, usual carriage – and head back into work as normal.

I work from home and don't have a commute, so for this microadventure I decided to seek out the most expensive commute in the country. Apparently those travelling between St Albans (a 'sought-after dormitory town', according to Wikipedia) and London during rush hour pay more per mile than anyone else. I would do this journey, but I'd do it differently. I would head north from the heart of London, but not by train. Somewhere close to St Albans I would find a spot where I could lay my head for the night and then in the morning I would join the commuters on their expensive train ride back into the city. This would allow me to compare how different the two journeys felt*.

'How would it feel to sit on that small hilltop and watch the trains rattling past? Where does that footpath beside the stream lead? What can you hear in that copse of trees when the sun sets and the birds settle down to roost?'

I hoped also to demonstrate that simply heading in a straight line out of any city will lead you, in just a couple of hours, to a pleasant patch of countryside. Convincing yourself of this will reassure you that you can get involved in microadventures no matter where you live, for it makes the country feel much more accessible.

At 5pm one evening I left my imaginary office by London Bridge – a central departure point chosen because this bridge was built by the Romans as part of the road I was now going to follow to St Albans. I was in The Shard, London's tallest skyscraper. Seeing as I was imagining myself to have an office, I thought it might as well be a top-floor penthouse office... It felt an incongruous place for a man with a backpack and a bivvy bag to be beginning a journey from. I gazed out from the 72nd floor, taking in the spectacular view. I wanted to establish a sense of how massive London is and how difficult it might be to get out of.

In a busy city it is easy to forget that somewhere out there are fields and rivers and peace. From the top of The Shard the city seemed to flow endlessly over the world, spilling all the way out to the horizon. I tried to follow the route of train tracks for as far as I could see them. Rather than taking the train out to that horizon I was now going to have to get out there by myself. I left The Shard and set off.

The first time you head out of town in search of a field to sleep in is a little daunting. I deliberately detoured via Tower Bridge and Big Ben and Buckingham Palace. These icons are so intrinsically linked to the heart of the city that they felt particularly removed from where I was hoping to get to.

I turned onto Watling Street, the old Roman road. Nowadays it is known as Edgware Road or just the A5. Head north along the Edgware Road, past London's old execution site, and you move into a different land. Middle Eastern groceries and restaurants line the street. My nose twitched as I passed kebab shops grilling chicken on hot coals. Red London buses trundled up and down, but the cinema I passed was showing films in Arabic. I was full of curiosity and enthusiasm.

Leaving a city in a straight line is like sucking a gobstopper in reverse. You begin at the central core and then pass through all the different layers, flavours and colours until eventually you arrive on the outside, seemingly a world away from where you began. Everything felt interesting on this warm summer evening. I drank it all in as the miles passed and the city gradually gave way to the first signs of suburbia.

'In a busy city it is easy to forget that somewhere out there are fields and rivers and peace.'

I had no idea how rural the trip to St Albans might be. The journey wasn't long: less than 30 miles. But I didn't know if there would be a swathe of greenbelt countryside or if it would be suburbs and business estates all the way, so I was pleased when I reached the first proper field north of London. I squeezed through a hedge and into the field. I wanted to stop for a moment and take a closer look. Standing in the field I felt relieved. I knew now that I would certainly be able to find a secluded, safe place to sleep. I wouldn't have to doss down round the back of a McDonald's somewhere.

The field stretched away from me for a hundred uncluttered metres, rising gently up a grassy slope to a cluster of large trees. I noticed how quiet it was in this field compared to where I began this small journey. The view opened out before me and was the furthest I had been able to see since leaving the top of The Shard. The oak trees were far smaller than The Shard, but they were also far older. I took a deep breath and inhaled the still air. Horizons are too close in cities.

Shortly afterwards I crossed the M25, the notorious motorway which is usually regarded as the outer limit of London. I was surprised how easy it had been to get out of London: leaving the city by car is always such a hassle.

I was only a few miles from St Albans now, so I decided to start looking for a place to sleep. The evening light was bright and golden, glinting through trees and lighting up a meadow of pale grass. I had a quick pint in a pub, then I bought a Chinese takeaway and turned off the road onto a riverside trail.

I was stunned. I could not believe what I found. A stream ran demurely through green water meadows. I know I have a tendency to harp on

about how easy it is to find hidden pockets of wildness. But even so, I could not believe how beautiful this little chalk stream was. I even found a clear, still pool where I could have a refreshing skinny dip, observed only by some disinterested cows. I certainly had not expected that on my commute from skyscraper to sought-after dormitory town. It was a delightful spot, the very epitome of seeking out fragments of beauty in built-up places.

Above the pool was a grassy hill, which I climbed to eat my spare ribs. The flat summit looked down over the river, fields and woods. A takeaway and an early night: this sounded like a typical weekday night for many a commuter. I lay on the grass and read my book for a while. Someone a mile or two to the west had even decided to celebrate my little microadventure by laying on a firework display for me. I fell asleep to the sound of crickets in the field and the soothing roar of the dual carriageway beyond the trees.

In the morning I would wake with the sun, follow the riverside footpath into St Albans, then hop on the fast train and roar back all the way I had just come – past the grassy knoll I was sleeping on, the pool I swam in, the fields and the Roman road. In 30 uninteresting, expensive minutes I would be back in the centre of London. It is as easy as that to switch between worlds.

So the next time you are on your commute, be sure to take a moment to look out of the window. The wild world out there is waiting for you to grasp it.

* An interesting and telling footnote. I had planned to use my time on the train back into London to look out of the window and observe how different my two journeys felt. I forgot. Instead I spent the whole journey looking at my phone and catching up on the cricket news from the previous day.
Note In case you need convincing that this is an achievable challenge for 'real' commuters with 'real' jobs and not just for lazy layabout authors like me, here are a couple of comments from a post on my blog:

Martin: Every day I sit on the train to work and watch the countryside go by and look oh so longingly at the woods – the woods, we gotta get into the woods!
AH: Why don't you walk home from work one night? You will see things from such a different perspective. And whenever you are on the train to work in the future you will have great memories of the microadventure...
Martin: Am taking your idea a step further and will wild camp the night in the woods that I see from my train.

Martin kept to his word, writing, 'I'm pleased to say the adventure went well and I spent a very enjoyable, and cosy, night.'

OTHER IDEAS LIKE THIS

➲ Walk the length of a Tube line or bus route you are familiar with.
➲ See pages 176–81 (M25) for more urban exploring.
➲ Use this book to plan other 5-to-9 adventures that fit into the working week.
➲ Stay on your train all the way to the end of the line and head home from there.
➲ Try this microadventure with a few colleagues from work. Take it in turns, once a month, to organise it along the route of each person's commute. Instantly you have several different microadventures and a few people to do them with. And you only have to organise one of them.
➲ Walk every street in your town or city. You have hundreds, even thousands, of miles of streets around you to discover and explore.

A JOURNEY AROUND YOUR HOME

Time Required:	From a few hours to a few days
Location:	Around your home
Means of Transport:	Up to you

I hit 'send' for the final time and turned off my computer. The end of another working day. It was only then that I decided to do this journey. I had nothing planned for that evening and the weather was fine, so I stuffed a sleeping bag, bivvy bag, Therm-a-Rest, water bottle and raincoat into a small bag. I slipped an apple into my pocket, grabbed my wallet and camera and left the house. My aim was to make a circle around my home, completing a lap at a sufficient distance from it so that I would complete the circle in time to get back to my desk for 9am the next day.

This idea appealed for a few reasons. It is cheap and pleasingly simple, and if it suddenly began to pour with rain I could just run back home. It would also help me explore the area around my home, discover new places and travel through familiar ones more slowly than I normally do. Even though I was not venturing far, I would be going to places I had never been. So I did need a map, but I could make do with the map app on my phone.

This microadventure was extremely easy. My circle was just 2½ miles from my front door, making a round trip of about 20 miles. But I was surprised how rewarding, refreshing and enjoyable it turned out to be, as well as how much I saw that was completely new to me. In fact, in terms of the effort versus reward ratio, this may well be the best microadventure in this book.

It is not the size of the journey that matters (as Xavier de Maistre demonstrated in 1790 by writing an entire book about a journey round his room), but the way you approach it. Another aspect of this idea is that you can repeat the journey without it becoming repetitive; increasing or decreasing the size of your circle, even just a little, will give you a completely new experience every time you try it. If you live in a city you probably will want to keep

the circle down to a size you can complete in a
single day.

The first thing that struck me as I walked out
from my house to the edge of my circle was just how
slowly I was travelling. I was walking a very familiar
route – I run here regularly but I had never pottered
down this road before. It seemed very different
at walking speed. It helped me understand a little
more why people enjoy dog walking (as I said 'good
afternoon' to an old chap walking his two bearded
terriers). There is an appealing rhythm to repeating
the same journey every single day and gradually
noticing how both the world and you are changing.
The slowness and the familiarity allow the brain
time to relax and meander. Indeed, a good addition
to this journey around your home would be to take
a photograph every hour, on the hour. It would
really help the process of slowing down, taking the
journey as it comes, and seeking beauty in the most
humdrum of settings.

I've hurtled through my youth in such a frenzied
hurry, always dissatisfied with the now, always
certain that the solution lies just beyond the
horizon, always pursuing it as fast as I can. Even
when I run I feel compelled to push myself hard,
feeling somehow that to enjoy the experience is
wrong and that if I'm not hurting and gasping and
on the verge of puking then I'm not doing it right.
So it was a novel feeling to be just strolling along.
Perhaps I'm getting old? Perhaps I'm growing up?

I climbed a hill and turned right at the top. I had
reached the perimeter of my circle. Now I would
follow it round until I arrived back here again in
the morning. I paused on the hilltop and looked
around. Clouds drifted steadily from left to right,
north to south. The cars on the main road below
crept nose to tail through the rush hour crush.

From up there I thought I could probably see the
whole route I was going to walk. It looked quite a
long way, an impressive distance to walk. In truth, I
knew I'd be back at my desk drinking tea first thing
in the morning. It wasn't really an epic voyage,
but it felt like one. In other words, it was a perfect
microadventure.

I strolled onwards, eating my Californian apple.
Horses grazed in a lush field beside a roaring road.

One drank from an old bath filled with water. Apple trees leant over the fence, the local fruits swelling and ripening. A pied woodpecker burst from one of the trees as I approached, the scarlet beneath its tail flashing as it flew.

The lottery of my chosen circle meant that I was fated to walk a couple of miles alongside the busy road. I wasn't particularly looking forward to it, but to my surprise I found it quite relaxing. The world was racing by and it helped emphasise my slowness.

I turned off the road by an old pub, closed down and ripe for demolition. The windows were boarded, the premises fenced off. Dandelions and saplings pushed through the cracked tarmac of the deserted car park, and sitting in the middle of it, shirt off and enjoying the evening sunshine, a rotund man casually read his newspaper. Life's rich tapestry...

It felt good now to be off the roads, following fields and footpaths. The air was filled with the distinctive aroma of summer evenings – of cut grass, willowherb and cow parsley. I detoured into

a small town for food. My feet were weary now and I was hungry. This was a little town that I visit regularly on errands, but entering it on foot, after hours of walking, made it feel different. It seemed more interesting than somewhere I could drive to in five minutes to go to the doctor or the butcher. I bought my food then returned to the fields to eat it.

I have done this so often around the world. The sensations of being hungry and weary and enjoying resting and eating are very familiar to me from my other adventures. Yet this was perhaps the strangest feeling of this microadventure so far, because it reminded me of one of my 'proper' journeys, faraway in the world, even though from the field where I was eating I could see a signpost to where I live. It felt surprisingly adventurous, refreshing and wild out there, just 2½ miles from home.

Night began to set in. But I decided to keep walking a little longer in order to savour the darkness. It had been a long, light summer but the nights were closing in now. This was the first real darkness I had experienced since summer settled

in. A choir was practising in a church. The door was open and I listened to them as I walked by.

In the darkness the known becomes the unknown. Even in this safe and familiar landscape I caught myself searching for a place to sleep, a sanctuary, like a fugitive or wild animal. It was odd to feel this so close to home. It was a reminder of how easy it is to step out of your comfort zone and to experience familiar things in an unfamiliar way.

I climbed a hill away from another small town and settled down to sleep at the edge of the wheat field up there. It was dark and deserted and peaceful. I could see city lights and a police car speeding through the night. Up there was a good place for a fugitive to hide, even one just temporarily fleeing from his computer and the madness of normal life.

In the early morning I sang 'Here Comes the Sun' as I do every single day when I'm on a trip and watching the sun rise. I sang it for the first time when cycling through the thin air and bitterly cold winter dawns of the high Andes 15 years ago, and I see no reason to stop now. So I sang as I walked, looking forward to breakfast. But as I was completing the last part of my circle the sky darkened and a summer rainstorm burst upon me. Almost instantly I was soaked. However, I was nearly home, so I knew I wouldn't be wet for long.

So I chose not to let the rain annoy me or get me down for 'there is nothing either good or bad, but thinking makes it so', as Shakespeare so rightly said. If you are able to persuade yourself to enjoy rain (sometimes easier said than done), then it can feel sublime, especially in summertime. The world was raw and primordial. It was a warm morning. The heavy rain plastered my hair and shirt. I felt more content than I had for weeks. In an hour or so I'd be changed and back at my desk, ready for just another ordinary working day, but this had been such an out of the ordinary beginning to my day. I smiled and picked up my pace for home.

THE CALCULATIONS

Perhaps you would like to give this idea a go yourself. School maths lessons may have been some time ago, so I'll help you out with the calculations! Where you live, how you travel, how hard you want to push yourself: these factors all determine the radius of the circle you'll choose to make. The formula you need to use is this: $2\pi r + 2r$ where 'r' is the radius of your circle, the distance you must travel from home before beginning the circle.

DISTANCE FROM HOME (MILES)	LENGTH OF YOUR JOURNEY (MILES)
1.	8.28
2.	16.57
3.	24.85
4.	33.13
5.	41.41
6.	49.70

YOU MIGHT ALSO WANT TO TRY

- Climb to your local high point and then travel to every prominent high point you can see around the horizon from there. (You might not want to attempt this lightly if you live in the Highlands. Or Nepal.)
- Do a short version of this in your lunch hour at work – follow your nose across town to the highest church spire you can see from your office. Take a photograph every five minutes if you want to really observe new places in your town.
- Challenge yourself to repeat the lap of your home every couple of months over the course of a year. Increase your circle's radius by a mile each time and you'll progress from an 8-mile stroll to a 50-mile hearty challenge by year's end.
- If circular journeys appeal, check out the Isle of Wight (pages 146–51) and M25 (pages 176–81).

⑨ CATCH IT, COOK IT, EAT IT

Britain can feel tame. The land has been managed and controlled for millennia. It has one of the highest population densities in the world.

Time Required:	One night
Difficulty Level:	Hard
Location:	Local
Essential Extra Kit:	Fishing gear. Reserve supply of food!

Even when we see a wild animal – a fox in the headlights, a startled deer bounding through a field at sunrise – it is within an environment moulded and dominated by humans. But underwater, things remain wild. Leaving aside our tendency to dam, divert and pollute, beneath the water's surface is still the domain of the creatures that live there.

This is one of the many reasons why I love rivers. Rivers, lakes, lochs and Britain's 11,000 miles of coastline provide an important connection to the wild world. There are endless ways to explore rivers (how I wish I'd had time to include an underwater journey in this book) and incorporate them into microadventures.

One way is by pitting your wits and skills against that wild world by trying to catch a fish. But don't cry 'humans interfering with nature, yet again!' I am suggesting fishing for food, not merely for fun. It certainly beats battery chickens, fish farms or resource-guzzling cattle. Consider it as a way of properly earning your evening fish and chips...

I sat on the riverbank with my friends Eliza and Chris while Andy* crept through the grass a few yards ahead of us – he not only had the permit and fishing rod, but he also actually knew how to wield the rod, unlike me.

We had come to enjoy a night out in the woods together. The plan was to catch our own supper (or, more accurately, for Andy to catch it) and cook it over a campfire. It was an idyllic idea. Andy had told me that he was a fantastic fisherman: I was looking forward to an imminent feast of fried trout.

There is something deeply relaxing about spending a couple of hours beside a river. Knowing that there are fat trout to outwit in those calm pools adds a spice of excitement too. It didn't really bother me that I wasn't actually doing the fishing; I still enjoyed being out there. I'd done this before, filling a pan with perch to cook with sorrel and wild mushrooms one warm evening in Sussex. But trout trumps perch any day...

'This is the slight downside of living like a hunter, of pitting yourself against the wild world. You do not always win.'

Trees hung low over the water. Swallows swirled and scythed the sky while swifts screamed and soared far above them. We laughed and chatted quietly. Andy prowled and cast over and over, the very study of concentration. The sun was low in the sky, reflecting gently from the babbling water. It was a perfect evening.

Perfect, except that we didn't catch anything.

This is the slight downside of living like a hunter, of pitting yourself against the wild world. You do not always win. Fortunately we had been sufficiently sceptical about Andy's prowess to bring along some other food, just in case. So we still cooked and camped in the woods, glad to be out in the fresh outdoors on one of the stillest, hottest nights of the year. This was a failed microadventure that felt anything but a failure.

ADVICE FOR RIVER ADVENTURES

➤ If you are aged 12 or over you need a licence to fish on a river or lake. Search online for the specific local one you require. No rod licence is needed for sea fishing.

➤ If it's the food aspect of this chapter that appeals, turn to pages 132–6 for a food microadventure.

➤ If you'd like more microadventures connected to rivers then try Coast to Coast – A Wild Journey (pages 66–9), A Journey from Source to Sea (pages 108–10) and River Swim (pages 80–3).

➤ For living off the land, see Back to Basics on pages 97–9.

* 'Andy' may (or may not) be a pseudonym to protect the identity and reputation of my shamed fisherman friend.

(10) ENTER A RACE

'50% icy terror, 50% fun,' was how I described my first lap of the race. I climbed wearily off my bike as my teammate zoomed away up the wet track, all fresh legs and enthusiasm. I was tired, shaken from a couple of crashes, and covered in mud. Someone handed me a hot, sweet mug of tea.

Time Required:	Between an hour and a weekend
Difficulty Level:	Up to you
Location:	Local
Means of Transport:	Foot or bicycle
Find Out More:	Watch the Video

Almost 24 hours later, my final lap felt more like 10% fun (because zooming downhill on a bike is always fun) and 90% exhaustion. After a day and a night of riding, the novelty of the 7-mile loop had somewhat worn off.

This was the Strathpuffer, one of Britain's toughest 24-hour mountain bike races. I was racing as part of a relay team of four. The Strathpuffer takes place in northern Scotland, in January. For 15 out of the 24 hours we raced through darkness.

The route began with a long climb up a track in a pine forest, slick with ice like a bobsled track. After the first 20 minutes of constant climbing, slipping and crashing, I absolutely hated the course. A skeleton, perched on a rusty bike, looked on as I cursed the leaden skies and the stupid, unrideable ice. However, the rest of the course compensated for the harsh winter conditions. There were stretches of technical rock slab to negotiate, a steep single-track

slalom through gorse bushes, and an exhilarating swoop down through a forest which provoked whoops of delight even at three in the morning. Or perhaps I should say 'especially' at three in the morning, as that's when madness really descends.

As the race progressed, much of the ice that had made the first hours so terrifying was scuffed from the trail. So mud replaced ice, night replaced day, then, after 15 long hours of night riding, day once again replaced night. And still we kept racing.

Music from the PA system kept spirits high throughout: the race had begun to Springsteen's 'No Retreat, No Surrender', followed by the equally apt 'A Little Less Conversation' (a little more action, please). In the evening a live band kept muddy legs tapping and stopped heavy eyelids from slipping closed as riders waited for their exhausted teammates to arrive and hand over the baton.

'In the evening a live band kept muddy legs tapping and stopped heavy eyelids from slipping closed as each rider waited for their exhausted teammate to arrive and hand over the baton.'

In between laps we drank tea, ate voraciously and compared horror stories of icy crashes and muddy punctures. The Strathpuffer has everything that I look for in an endurance race: it is tough and a bit daft, it takes place in a beautiful landscape, and even the most hardcore of competitors is self-deprecating and humble.

I was acutely conscious of the absurdity of what we were all doing. Hundreds of mud-caked, cake-fuelled idiots were just riding round and round in circles in a forest while the rest of the world enjoyed their Saturday night followed by a Sunday morning lie-in. But as the clock ticked over to 24 hours and the race ended, the waves of weariness were replaced by a warm feeling of satisfaction and camaraderie. And a deep yearning for my bed. It had been a harsh but fabulous 24 hours doing something new and difficult, in a beautiful landscape with friends new and old.

'There were stretches of technical rock slab to negotiate, a steep single-track slalom through gorse bushes, and an exhilarating swoop down through a forest which provoked whoops of delight even at three in the morning.'

Entering a race like this is a memorable weekend microadventure, and there are plenty of options as Britain is blessed with hundreds of similar events throughout the year. It doesn't matter whether it's a 24-hour race or a 5km park run that feels like a challenge for you; it's just important to try something. To do something difficult that will serve as a stepping stone towards other, bigger adventures. The rewards of entering a race are well worth the pain of being so stiff that you can hardly walk up the office stairs on Monday morning.

TIPS FOR YOUR FIRST RACE

Microadventures are not just for those who enjoy camping out. The concept applies for anyone willing to try new things and break out of boring ruts. Saying that it is 'important to get out of your comfort zone' is a tired cliché, but it is true and it is important.

Events that are already organised are the simplest to commit to, and as committing is by far the hardest part of any adventure, entering a race is a simple way of starting off. Do this once or twice and perhaps you'll be tempted to try a bigger and bolder adventure.

Races are also excellent because they cater for every capability. Everyone can push themselves to their very limits in a race, whether it be a 5km run in the local park, an ultramarathon across a desert, or a 24-hour mountain bike race. Don't be put off from entering a race because you won't win: I've never won a race in my life. Enter a race just for fun, for a challenge and to get you to actually do something.

The Strathpuffer illustrates this well. I entered the Quads division, which is the least taxing as you share the burden with three teammates, alternating laps throughout the 24 hours. If that is too easy you can enter as a pair. And if you are really hard, enter as a single, looping round and round by yourself, without stopping, for 24 gruelling hours. But even that is too easy for some people: a mad minority ride the Strathpuffer on single-speed bikes – bikes without gears! There will always be somebody dafter than you, whatever you attempt!

This is not a book to help you train and prepare for a race, but the following advice will help you get to the finish line, regardless of the standard of fitness and equipment you arrive at the start line with.

Pace Yourself. Don't bow to peer pressure or some inner-macho-masochist and set off too fast. I guarantee you will ignore this, particularly if you are male. But try to ease into the rhythm of the race steadily, and to just run your own race. Unless you are planning to win (in which case this chapter is not for you), then you are only racing against yourself – either to finish with a personal best time or simply to finish. It's silly to try to match the pace of other people when you have no idea about their ability.

Drink Plenty. Make sure you drink lots of water before, during and after the race. You don't need to go crazy, but taking regular sips of water is a good idea. If you feel thirsty it is too late: you are already dehydrated.

Eat Lots. This applies to long races rather than short events. In long races it is important to get into the habit of eating regularly to keep your energy levels high. With races of just a few hours' duration you can get by with energy gels, drinks and water. For longer races you will probably want to try foods such as nuts, raisins, biltong, flapjacks and bananas. Eating a variety of foods helps you get a range of carbohydrate, protein and fat as well as important minerals. The key thing is to practise eating during your longer training sessions to see what agrees with your stomach in a long race. If it goes wrong the consequences can be unpleasant...

If you are now encouraged to tackle a race, have a look at findarace.com or if you fancy attempting an ultramarathon then visit www.ultramarathonrunning.com/races/uk.html

OTHER RACE IDEAS

Britain has so many mad races. Examples include the Isle of Man's 'Race the Sun' (a 100-mile relay lap of the island between sunrise and sunset), the 145-mile Grand Union Canal Race, the 95-mile West Highland Way Race, or the 'self-transcendence' race of running round and round

a running track in Tooting Dec for 24 hours! The crew at www.findarace.com have picked these as their favourite races to try in the UK:

➲ Man vs Mountain
www.ratracemanvsmountain.com
A 20-mile run to the summit of Snowdon and back down. Several obstacles thrown in along the way, including abseiling and deep water crossings.

➲ Dart 10K
www.outdoorswimmingsociety.com
A 10km swim down the River Dart in Devon. Described not as a race but a journey, with swimmers going at their own pace. Outdoor swimming's equivalent to a marathon.

➲ Buttermere Triathlon
www.highterrainevents.co.uk/18.html
Quite possibly Britain's most scenic triathlon. A 1.5km swim in Buttermere Lake, a 44km road bike course taking in Honister Pass, and a 10km trail run around the shores of Crummock Water.

➲ Dunwich Dynamo
www.londonschoolofcycling.co.uk/content.php?id=18
A 200km night ride from London to the Suffolk Coast. Held on the Saturday night nearest a full moon in July. Free event, just turn up and ride.

➲ Red Bull Steeplechase
www.steeplechase.redbull.co.uk
A 21-mile knockout race through the heart of the Peak District. Race between four steeples with the slowest section of the field being eliminated at each steeple.

➲ Howies Coed Y Brenin Enduro
www.summitcycles.co.uk/enduro
1,000 riders take part in a mass-start mountain bike endurance challenge.

11 AN OUT OF OFFICE EXPERIENCE

Rain rattled the window. Keyboards rattled behind me. Strip lights hummed and flickered. The radio played quietly in the corner. I was here to take three office workers on their first microadventure.

Time Required:	One night
Difficulty Level:	Medium – because of planning and cooking equipment required, not because of the trip itself
Location:	Close to where you work
Essential Extra Kit:	Clean clothes to change into when you get back to work
Find Out More:	Watch the Video

While I waited for them to finish their work, I watched an elderly man urge his mobility scooter a little faster across the wet grey car park below us. I sighed. I have slept many nights in a bivvy bag but was reluctant to add to my tally in this weather. The three guys I had come to meet had never slept in a bivvy bag and looked a little reluctant to start now.

But we persisted. And that is the key to doing almost anything interesting in life. You've just got to get out there and do it. So we began.

Nigel, Tony, Colin and I pedalled through damp grey streets and a heavy rain shower or two. We dropped down the high street and out of town. In a small town, escape is easy, either on foot or by bike. In a city, just take the train. It's easy to get out of town whichever way you do it. The only difficult part is getting round to it.

The rain stopped as we left the town for the fresh air and brighter skies of the countryside. The sun even began to shine. Wet hedgerows sparkled in the evening sunshine. We pedalled hard and cheered out loud at the simple pleasure of racing down a quiet road towards the coast.

The roads narrowed. Overhanging trees closed in above us. We turned off the tarmac and rode along a bridleway laden with autumn blackberries. Up and over a hill we went. Then we were racing like mad little things, down a curving, narrow path, down, down all the way to the sea. I went flying over my handlebars and landed in a bush. Everyone laughed. We dashed on. And we were just in time. The sky was heavy and grey, the sea had a strange purple sheen, but between the sea and the sky blazed a brilliant red sunset. A few minutes after we arrived it disappeared beneath the horizon. We were so happy to be out there, making the very most of Now.

Seals bobbed quietly below our clifftop vantage. Colin observed that getting here from the office had taken the same length of time as his usual daily drive home. He had swapped his boring commute for a bike ride, a fabulous sunset and a sea view. We unrolled bivvy bags in a grassy hollow on top of the cliffs. For tonight at least, this was home. We were sheltered from the wind but open to the sea and the stars. We ate and drank and chatted.

I lay awake for a while, watching the stars and a distant lighthouse's regular rhythm. Thankfully it did not rain in the night. We woke warm and well-rested at sunrise. Chatter bubbled amongst us about the strange and unusual experience of sleeping under the stars without a tent. It's a powerful experience the first time you try it, it really is. Add an espresso and a bacon sandwich, a swim in the sea and a fast bike ride to work and you have a happy start to a working day.

MILTON KEYNES MICROADVENTURE

Some time later I repeated this experiment with people from a different office. An anonymous grey warehouse on a Milton Keynes business estate was another unlikely place to have come for a microadventure. Again I waited while they finished work – more call-centre headsets, pot plants and strip lights. But then we busted out into some surprisingly enjoyable and scenic mountain bike trails, racing the fast-fading spring light a few miles out of town. We carried small rucksacks with our bivvy equipment. It turned dark early and the night was cold, so we earmarked a field to sleep in and then spent the evening in a nearby pub, spilling out merrily after last orders to sleep.

The night was noisy with foxes and rabbits. The dawn was frosty and cold and beautiful like a Constable painting. We were not anywhere exotic, just in a fallow field beside a canal. The fast intercity train into London roared past every 20 minutes. But rather than being annoying, that noisy train was a reminder of how small a step it is from commuting routine to a night in the wild. A tiny step, but a memory that will linger for a long time.

The frost gleamed on the grass as the sun rose wanly beyond the low, drifting gossamer mist. And as we cycled back to town, riding fast to warm ourselves, Andy called out to me that, 'This could be about the best thing I've done in a very long time. I'm really happy.'

 A GLASGOW NIGHT OUT

Keen to evangelise the idea of adventuring in your 5-to-9 – those 16 precious hours of daily freedom – I knew that I needed to venture beyond my own circle of friends and acquaintances.

Time Required:	One night
Difficulty Level:	Pretty easy
Location:	Anywhere you want
Optional Extra Kit:	Binoculars - it's fun to look back at the city you ordinarily live in

After all, perhaps my friends who like sleeping on a hill are weird and not representative of normal people?! I also wanted to introduce microadventures to other people and see how they got on. So I found some volunteers on Twitter

(via the hashtag #microadventure) and then headed to Glasgow, a city I did not know, to try something new with some people I had never met. I hoped that it would demonstrate how easy it is to have a microadventure and how little equipment, planning or expertise you need.

My train pulled into Glasgow at 5 o'clock. It was easy, even in rush hour in a busy train station, to find my fellow microadventurers: they were the only other people wearing backpacks who did not appear to be in a tearing hurry. There were five of us: three guys and two girls. We had never met, we knew nothing about each other, and quite possibly the only thing we had in common would be a willingness to spend a night on top of a hill with a handful of strangers – we would find out soon enough! I'm not naturally inclined to seek out people I don't already know, but I have really enjoyed all the microadventures that I have done with new people.

The aim of our microadventure was to keep it simple and keep it local. Together we boarded a train crammed with commuters and said our hellos as we rattled and clunked slowly out of the city. We were on our way to the nearest decent-sized hills. To minimise the complications of equipment and logistics we would eat dinner in a pub at the foot of the fells. We'd be back down again in time

for breakfast. So we needed minimal equipment. Going to the pub also gave us a chance to get to know each other a bit better over a beer and a burger before we headed up the hill.

The girls, Claire and Shannon, were students. They both enjoyed the outdoors but had never slept in a bivvy bag before. Psychologically it is a very different experience to a night in a tent, but a tent's illusion of being protected and being indoors is actually the primary reason why I advocate experiencing a night in a bivvy bag. The girls were excited about trying something new. Stuart had more experience of this sort of thing: he used to enjoy planning and heading off on long trips into the mountains. But now he found himself working long shifts as a police officer. He also had a young daughter so struggled to find time to get up into the hills any more. Stuart hoped that this microadventure would give him ideas for quick fixes of fresh air and solitude that were compatible with his busy life.

'We had never met, we knew nothing about each other, and quite possibly the only thing we had in common would be a willingness to spend a night on top of a hill with a handful of strangers.'

Chris, the fifth member, was an experienced and active outdoorsman. He actually lived right at the foot of the hills we were about to climb, so for him this would be a good reminder not to overlook the countryside closest to your home when seeking a short microadventure fix. Just because it is near by does not mean it is boring.

The evening weather was glorious as we left the pub and walked through a wood carpeted with bluebells. We passed the final houses and turned onto the hill. I enjoyed walking past the homes as they helped emphasise the slight barminess of what we were doing. Five strangers with perfectly good homes, soft beds and fluffy pillows were choosing instead to spend the night together on a hill. The sun was low and dazzled our eyes as we walked. The land glowed a soft shade of honey. Lambs were fattening up in the lush fields. We felt lucky to be out there.

Although compared to most people I have a low-stress life, I still experience a physical feeling of relaxation when I get away like this. It is a rinsing away of the residual build-ups of stress and frustration. When I head into the hills I feel, very distinctly, a lightness in my step and a release of pressure all over my body. I breathe more easily. I believe several factors contribute to this: being somewhere new away from places I associate with stress or boredom, being unable to address (and therefore less inclined to worry about) all the busy, annoying stuff life demands, a slowing down in my pace of thought, and the simple pleasures of fresh air, natural scenery and physical exercise.

Shannon told us that although she had often been camping with her family she had never headed up a hill at sunset like this. She had never been in the wild at night. She was wearing jeans, a lumberjack shirt and Timberland boots and looked like she was off to Glastonbury rather than up a hill. You wouldn't want to climb a serious mountain equipped like her, but a small grassy hill in the springtime is fine. Her family thought she was mad coming here tonight, she said, grinning broadly.

The track petered out and now we had to climb straight up the steep hill. We gradually stopped talking, saving our breath until we reached the summit, where we shared a bag of sweets and admired the view. It was spectacular.

There was nobody else up on those windy hills. The sun was setting, leaving the world to darkness and to us. Lochs gleamed like pools of quicksilver in the west. But my eyes were drawn more strongly southwards, towards the city we had left behind.

The lights began to twinkle from the tower blocks. 'The long day wanes, the slow moon climbs. Come my friends: 'tis not too late to seek a newer world.' This was no *Odyssey*, but right now the light was extraordinary. The view was genuinely beautiful. The city filled the plain. A full moon hung in the sky. From above, cities appear more like an encampment set temporarily within an ancient and permanent landscape than you ever realise when you are actually in them. The glow from a million orange streetlights reflected on the clouds above the silent streets. Stuart, the police officer, pointed out the area of Glasgow where he worked. He assured me that tonight the streets down there would be anything but silent. He was looking forward to a peaceful night up here away from his usual customers!

Lights flowed across the plain like volcanic lava. So much of our countryside is smeared with sodium orange lights. It is a real pity that we consider this normal and that it often takes effort to seek out darkness and stars... My ponderings were interrupted by Chris chuntering loudly to himself as he realised he'd forgotten his toothbrush.

We dropped a little way down from the summit to shelter from the wind, searching for little flat patches among the tussocks of grass. The night was cold now and we wrapped up as warmly as we could. Claire declared this to be heaven before we all settled to silent contemplation and then sleep.

The first sound in the morning was a skylark singing above our heads. You could not ask for a better alarm clock. Poor Shannon woke very early with the dawn and then could not go back to sleep. She watched the sunrise from the edge of the cliffs. There is no denying that you get a better night's sleep in your own bed. But our entire group, to my delight, declared that they would like to do this again sometime, despite us having underestimated how chilly the night was going to be.

The relative discomfort of a night like this is amply compensated by the feeling of walking out of the hills in the bright early morning sunshine.

If I was at home I would still be asleep. This was a better beginning to the day.

I walked up a hill with strangers and came down with friends. For some of our little group, drawn together only by Twitter, the experience had been nothing less than a microadventure epiphany. Stuart described it as the best commute he had ever had.

And that's it. That's the way to look at this – not as a big, complicated hassle of an adventure, but as something you can do on a normal, commuting weekday. Because in no time at all we were back at the station, then back into the city and swallowed up by the busy world once more.

DREAM BIG, START SMALL, SHARE YOUR STORY

For busy people short on time, keeping your plans small and unambitious can actually be a way of getting you outdoors *more* often than trying to plan a big adventure and ending up frustrated by a lack of time, incompatible diaries or unamused partners.

By all means dream of big adventures and begin planning to make them happen. But why not concoct the smallest possible distillation of your big idea and begin with that? If you want to cycle round the world, first try cycling across England. If you want to climb K2, begin with some local hills. If you want to walk to the North Pole, see if you can hack walking across your county.

If you want to get in touch with other people who are interested in microadventures, use the hashtag #microadventure to search online. Whilst a few people have criticised me for putting a fancy name and a hashtag to activities that people have always done – camping, cycling, floating down rivers on tractor tyres – I think the 'community' aspect of microadventure is one of its greatest assets. I know hardened ramblers who hate the term 'microadventure' will recoil even more at me using the term 'community'. But a hashtag is a powerful way of helping people find others not only with similar interests and passions, but also similar concerns and limitations posting fabulous photographs of sunrises on a hilltop. It gives 'ordinary' people the confidence to think 'I could do that too. And not only that, I *will* do that.'

So search the social media site of your choice for #microadventure. Or, if that sentence either leaves you blank or makes you angry, go to the library and read *The Gentle Art of Tramping* instead.

13

COAST TO COAST –
AN ANCIENT JOURNEY

Living in a big city it is easy to forget about adventure, or to look up and see the clouds racing across the skies tonight, or forget the changing seasons and the trees budding in the springtime.

Time Required:	2 days+
Difficulty Level:	Medium
Location:	Northern England
Means of Transport:	Bicycle
Essential Extra Kit:	Sustrans' map of Route 72
Find Out More:	Watch the Video

But despite sometimes feeling like you are living inside a hermetically sealed cocoon, you are never far from adventure – if only you choose to seek it out. Just a couple of hours' ride or walk from any city will take you to somewhere new, to somewhere wild, to somewhere beautiful.

Any journey that begins and ends at the sea feels satisfying. I looked out across the North Sea, waiting for sunrise. The cold brown water reflected the sky's extravagant reds and purples. This was a dawn for a Pacific island, not for a winter's day on the north-east coast of England.

My pleasure was offset slightly because I was already wearing all of my clothes, including those I was due to sleep in tonight, and I was absolutely

If you want to cycle with no traffic at all, search online about Britain's 4,500 miles of disused railway lines that have been converted into walking and cycling paths. You are also allowed to cycle on bridleways (marked as the long green dashes on Ordnance Survey maps).

The Mountain Bothies Association is a charity which maintains about 100 shelters in some of the remoter parts of the UK. If you like the idea of bothies, please consider volunteering some time to help with their renovation work or make a donation. Most bothies are in Scotland (lovely ones include Meanach, Shenavall, 'The Hutchy' hut, Suileag, Culra, Rubha Hunish, Kearvaig, and Maol Bhuidhe), but other gems include Grwyne Fawr and Cwm Dulyn in Wales and the Haughton Green bothy that I stayed in in Northumberland. Always leave them cleaner than you found them. Take in your own wood wherever possible. Re-stock the wood pile. And make sure to tell your tale in the Bothy book.

You could concoct an interesting coast-to-coast route between Scotland's bothies. The Mountain Bothies Association's website has a useful map for hatching plans (www.mountainbothies.org.uk).

The World Heritage List includes 28 properties in the United Kingdom, forming part of the cultural and natural heritage which the World Heritage Committee considers as having outstanding universal value. If you rode between all of those it would be an enormous and fascinating journey.

BRITAIN'S LONG-DISTANCE CHALLENGES

Britain is blessed with many established long-distance challenges. Whilst I think the best adventures are those you invent for yourself, these footpaths and well-known routes will help you dream up your own personal challenge. Search online for the National Trails or Scotland's Great Trails. Examples include:

- Cleveland Way
- Cotswold Way
- Glyndŵr's Way
- Hadrian's Wall Path
- North Downs Way
- Offa's Dyke Path
- Peddars Way and Norfolk Coast Path
- Pembrokeshire Coast Path
- Pennine Bridleway / Pennine Way
- The Ridgeway
- South Downs Way
- South West Coast Path
- Thames Path
- Yorkshire Wolds Way

The Long Distance Walker's Association is a great resource. Feel free to replace the word Walker with Runner...

Other noted challenges include the Fred Whitton Challenge and the Ramsay's Round, the Yorkshire Three Peaks, The Dartmoor Ten Tors, The Welsh 3,000s and the South Downs by Mountain Bike (or do it there and back if that is too easy. It's even been done there and back and there again!).

For many people a goal that runs on for years is to gradually 'bag' all 282 'Munros' (a mountain higher than 3,000 feet) or 221 of the slightly lower 'Corbetts'. Once you've done that, and then done it with bivvying on each of the summits, you can move on to the 2,000 'Marilyns': British hills of over 150 metres. In other words, there are more ideas and challenges than you will ever need.

COAST TO COAST – A WILD JOURNEY

14

Time Required:	6 days
Location:	Northern Scotland
Difficulty Level:	Hard
Essential Extra Kit:	Packraft
Find Out More:	Watch the Video

Rannoch Moor appeared even more foreboding than usual. The ground was thick with snow this year. The sky was grey, low and threatening. Burns and rivers had frozen solid. They wound motionless round the base of black mountains marbled with ice. The only sign of life was the herd of magnificent stags that had made their way down from the ridge in search of fodder. They steamed and snorted in the bitter afternoon air.

Our excitement rose at the sight of such wilderness from the train window. But would the river – 'our river' – be frozen too? Andy and I

chewed over the possibilities and marvelled that a landscape such as this could be just hours away from the city landscape we had sleepily departed on the early train. But we had transformed too. From boarding the train in London clutching skinny cappuccinos (Andy, not me) and *The Guardian* (me, not Andy), to a new mindset poring over map contours and trying to estimate how much tougher this weather was going to make things.

We heaved heavy packs onto eager shoulders and climbed down from the train. The station was deserted. We began walking east. The plan was simple: to cross Scotland. We would walk from the west coast to the River Spey. Then we'd inflate the packrafts we were carrying (a grown-ups' version of a rubber dinghy) and paddle downstream to the sea.

We filled our water bottles from a bouncing stream (the warmer, wetter west coast was not frozen) and pitched our tent in a gnarled, lichen-covered wood. Mammoth gusts of wind raged against the tent and heavy rain battered us throughout the night. This far north it falls dark by 4pm in January and is not light again until 8am, so at least we had plenty of time to sleep.

For the first couple of days we would travel cross-country, trusting to deer tracks to steer us through the steep, heather-covered wilderness. We scrambled up and down slopes, pushing through thickets and crossing racing streams. Progress was slow and our laden packs weighed us down. A splendid stag followed us for half a mile just 20 metres away while we climbed a narrowing glen topped with snowy crags. All around us was silence. For two days we did not see a human, a vehicle or even a light. The sense of challenging adventure and genuine solitude right here in Britain was intoxicating. I felt uplifted, at peace and inspired in a way I rarely do out in the 'real world'. I was not fretting about my work, my bank balance or future ambitions. Out there I was able to just live in the present and to relish it.

We pitched camp beside a loch at the confluence of two imperious glens. Our tent looked tiny in the giant theatre formed by the striking peaks that rose above us. At dawn we emerged from the tent into star-strewn darkness. The silhouette of the mountains reflected onto the still water of the loch.

More cross-country scrambling took us up and over a ridge and down to a dark rippling stream. A buzzard circled overhead. We tramped along the headwaters of the stream. From its soggy marsh beginning, this stretch of water turned quickly to a precocious little burn fringed with watercress. Soon it was 3-foot wide, 4, 5, 6... and I was beginning to itch for the boats. With every spidery tributary that joined the stream the water grew slightly deeper and the volume of flow increased. I crossed my fingers that we would be able to take to the water soon.

At last the water was deep enough. I was excited like a kid at Christmas as we inflated the packrafts.

We lashed our rucksacks to the front of the boats, then off we went. The water took hold of us and carried us merrily downstream. Whoopee! Yeehah! Free motion! We paddled round meanders, through dark, deep patches, over riffles of golden gravel and past rocky clusters. We drifted quietly past deer and watched tiny dippers flitting upstream. Andy and I grinned at each other and agreed that this beat walking with those infernal heavy packs.

'We heaved heavy packs onto eager shoulders and climbed down from the train. The station was deserted. We began walking east. The plan was simple: to cross Scotland.'

Ahead of us loomed the first set of rapids. We held on to the river bank and discussed what to do.

'Shall we recce it?' I proposed.

'Recce is for wimps!' declared Andy and launched himself into the white water*. The run was short but exhilarating and we laughed and whooped when we emerged at the bottom.

We were both sad when the river's path diverged from our own and we had to continue once more on foot.

Unfortunately Andy injured his knee so we then had to hitchhike to reach the River Spey. In 'proper' expeditions this would be frowned upon. Microadventures, however, are about accepting whatever compromises are necessary in order to squeeze as much adventure as you can into your own particular circumstances. It doesn't matter what other people think.

Dawn was pink behind the white peaks of the Cairngorms as we inflated the boats once again on the bank of the Spey. Small icebergs floated by. I'd never seen icebergs on a British river before! I was excited about paddling but I was nervous about taking to the water in such cold weather.

The slow parts of the current were frozen solid, adding to the sense of trepidation. I thought about how little I fancied dying trapped beneath the ice. I was conscious of how dangerous the coming days could be, as well as being fun and challenging.

My hands were painfully cold within minutes. It was apparent that neither of us were wearing sufficient clothes and all day we teetered on the brink of falling seriously cold. Mighty slabs of ice, the size of pool tables and ten inches thick, were jumbled on top of each other along the banks. Some were grey and stuck through with sticks and pebbles, others shining and transparent. Overhanging tree branches dangled detritus a metre above the current water level, a reminder of the recent storms. Low clouds skimmed the sky. The wan white sun gave only an illusion of warmth.

Beneath the bridge where the A9 crossed the Spey the whole river was frozen solid, jammed with a backlog of ice floes. We had to walk alongside the river, hauling our boats behind us. Would we be able to paddle any more of this journey? Pairs of ducks flew overhead with anxious purpose and skeins of geese drifted high across the winter sky. Loch Insh opened up before us, and that too was

frozen. We walked the length of the loch, fearing that our trip was doomed. But, thankfully, the loch's outflow lifted our spirits: there was a steady flow of water from beneath the frozen loch surface. We were back in the game!

It was still bitterly cold, though, so I put my gloved hands inside plastic bags and that helped ease the agony of burning cold. My feet and bum, wedged immobile in the bottom of a wet boat, alternated between being numb and aching painfully. Each evening we were so grateful for the warmth of our sleeping bags and the cheery roar of the camping stove.

The highlight of the river was a morning of rapids. They sluiced down past the distinctive aroma of the Knockando whisky distillery, whose straw-coloured malt sits beside me as I type these words.

Rivers change their mood as they move along the journey. The river later slowed and became beautiful and majestic where wealthy homes and increasingly smart fishing huts lined the banks.

From there the Spey races eagerly towards its end. We swept quickly down into the estuary, watching a tree slide down the bank into the river followed by a roaring landslide of rocks and

ALTERNATIVE COAST-TO-COAST JOURNEYS

Travelling from one coast to another is always satisfying. It is such a clear-cut journey, with a significant start point and a very obvious, tangible conclusion. Whether you are skateboarding across Australia, cycling the Race Across America or merely pottering across our sceptred (yet small) isle in a weekend, the feeling of satisfaction when you first see the sea still remains. Here are a few alternative coast-to-coast trips.

- Crossing England by mountain bike from Whitehaven to Sunderland. The CTC has resources and maps for this.
- The South West peninsula. Begin on the north coast of Devon or Cornwall and head south. Following the River Dart or the Tamar would be an enjoyable route.
- Tackle the length of Wales in the legendary Dragon's Back Race down the country's mountainous spine.
- The TGO Challenge (The Great Outdoors Challenge). Hiking and wild camping across Scotland is definitely worth doing, for the scenery, the fun of planning, and the camaraderie.
- Beginning on the west coast of England, close to Bristol, you can paddle canals and rivers all the way to the Thames, London and the sea. (See pages 111–13 for an introduction to the Devizes to Westminster canoe marathon.)

dirt. An otter struggled to haul a flapping salmon from the water. Diving cormorants and circling seagulls were clues that the end was approaching. We paddled past seals as they waited for salmon coming in on the tide. They flopped from the bank down into their pool and raised their curious heads to check on our strange crafts. Muddy brown waves crashed ahead of us: we had reached the North Sea. We hauled the boats out of the water for the last time and climbed up a noisy shingle beach. We had crossed Scotland.

I fingered a smooth round pebble and slipped it into my pocket, a souvenir of a magnificent adventure. Then we packed away the boats, heaved our packs onto our backs, and walked off to catch a bus home.

* No: reconnaissance is for *sensible people*. Please do not approach your own river journeys in the same way as us!

15 A CREDIT CARD ADVENTURE

I love the Tour de France and I love Yorkshire, but I never imagined that one day the Tour de France would begin in Yorkshire.

Time Required:	A weekend
Difficulty Level:	Medium
Location:	Yorkshire
Means of Transport:	Bicycle
Essential Extra Kit:	Credit card, yellow jersey

It seemed an unlikely combination. But it also seemed a great excuse to go for a bike ride.

Cycling's popularity has surged in recent years. Huge numbers of people now enjoy a long ride on a Saturday morning, and perhaps another on Sunday too if the weather is kind. Country lanes across the land are crowded with the species known as the 'MAMIL' (Middle-aged Man in Lycra), an often overweight beast, under-dressed and riding an overly-expensive bike.

Popular also for many years has been the idea of credit card cycle touring. For people who like the idea of a cycle tour but prefer the idea of a hotel to a bike laden with a tent, this is a very pleasant way to travel. After all, racing bike plus toothbrush plus credit card plus hotel surely makes a lot of sense!

For this microadventure I was looking to combine different things. I wanted to do two consecutive day rides and get the excitement of riding fast on an unburdened bike, but I did not want to be restricted to looping round the familiar area that I am able to cover in a single day. I wanted the lightness of travel and the lack of clutter that appeals to credit card tourists. With twisted arm (and only in the interests of this book, you understand), I was willing to endure the decadent luxury of grazing my way

from cafe to pub. But I also wanted to hold on to the delicious freedom of proper cycle touring. So I would carry a bivvy bag in order that I could sleep wherever nightfall found me.

I planned to combine the best bits of all these kinds of cycling along the first stage of the Tour de France, circling for 120 miles around the Yorkshire Dales from Leeds to Harrogate. I climbed onto my bike outside a Greggs bakery in Leeds city centre. The aroma of Steak Bake pasties filled the air. It was difficult to imagine the world's greatest annual sporting event beginning here. Across the road was the Victorian town hall. I waited for a large young lady with a double pushchair and a cream bun to pass then I took the first pedal strokes on my

that a bird of prey was gliding parallel to me, cruising at more than 25mph. I heroically saw off attacks from the combined ranks of Bradley Wiggins and Chris Froome and Lance Armstrong and Miguel Indurain. All glory was mine! But what's this? Disaster strikes! A red traffic light and a stern-looking lollipop lady put paid to my dash for glory. I squeezed my brakes and slowed to a stop.

As I pedalled through peaceful villages or paused to let dairy cows cross the road, I enjoyed imagining the same rural scene blaring with all the razzmatazz and colour of the Tour de France. I inhaled the summer smells of pink roadside willowherb and the mown hay in the meadows.

At Skipton the route headed north into the beautiful Yorkshire Dales National Park, where the road narrows and becomes hemmed in by dry stone walls. Storm clouds brewed overhead but the evening sunshine was warm. I crossed my fingers that the rain would hold off.

I was hungry. But I was also keen to eat up some of the 120 miles that lay ahead of me. Each village appeared more picturesque and appealing than the last one. Each had a pub, tempting me to stop in and call it a day. I kept pushing on until Kettlewell, when I succumbed, ready to embrace the world of credit card cycle touring. Beer in the sunshine. Fish and chips. Another beer. Sunshine on my face. One more beer? If you insist... This is how the Tour de France should be!

I rode a short distance out of the village to sleep. I hid my bike behind a wall and climbed the steep hill beside the road.

Cycling shoes are not ideal for this.

But even so, within 15 sweaty, grunting minutes I was high above the road and alone for the night. It is always worth making a little effort to find a special spot to sleep because the memories and the smug Instagram photo last long after you've got your breath back. Bivvying in rural spots is even easier than finding a B&B for the night – it is the simplest, most relaxing accommodation there is. The views and atmosphere trump a 5-star hotel,

Tour de France debut: a momentous moment for any cyclist.

I soon left Leeds behind and entered the more bucolic landscapes of Harewood and the Wharfe valley. It was just an ordinary day out on my bike, but because I was following the route of the Tour de France I viewed everything through different eyes. As I hunched down low to pick up speed on the downhills, I found myself daydreaming like a child. I was hurtling along at race pace, at the head of a spectacular breakaway. The crowds were cheering! Those pretty girls with the stuffed toy lions on the podium were preparing to give me the yellow jersey and a big kiss. The commentators were marvelling at my effortless talent. I noticed

although I will admit that the bed is a little less comfortable and the mini bar is BYO.

The valley below was chequered with bright green fields, dry stone walls and stone barns. The River Wharfe reflected the blues and golds of the sunset sky. The only sounds were the sheep calling to each other up and down the valley and the loud call of a green woodpecker in the tree above me. The evening was so still that when the woodpecker flew away, undulating across the sky, I could hear its wings whirring.

'As I pedalled through peaceful villages or paused to let dairy cows cross the road, I enjoyed imagining the same rural scene blaring with all the razzmatazz and colour of the Tour de France.'

I was travelling as lightly as I could manage for this trip. This meant absolutely no spare clothes and a bin bag for a raincoat. A disadvantage of travelling this light is having nothing to use as a pillow. So I stripped naked (another benefit of being alone on a hilltop), bundled my clothes up for a pillow, and climbed into my sleeping bag.

A bird of prey (I'm ashamed that I don't know what it was) called to its young in their nest before swooping in to feed them. The same bird woke me in the night, calling loudly and repeatedly from a branch just a few feet above my head. I lay motionless, entranced. It was so close. Did it know I was there? Was it going to swoop down and peck my eyes? Unlikely, of course, and quite a silly thought when I see it written down, but in the dark I definitely felt that *I* was in *its* domain. The night always feels wild when you're in a bivvy bag on a hilltop.

The annual Perseid meteor shower was passing overhead that night and I was looking forward to an excellent view of the shooting stars in the dark skies of the Dales. I gazed up at the sky to

wait for the show to begin. But the next thing I knew, it was dawn: 50 miles on the bike and an evening in a pub meant I had no trouble falling asleep. I woke to drizzle on my face and a soupy world of grey cloud. This was not the splendid emerald-green world I had left behind. The drizzle was annoying and threatened to splash me to complete and irritable wakefulness, so I buried deeper down into my bivvy bag and went back to sleep.

When I woke again the sun had risen above the fells, the clouds had rolled away and their only trace was a rainbow straddling the valley and bright jewels of water shining on the grass around me. It was going to be a fabulous day.

'When I woke again the sun had risen above the fells, the clouds had rolled away and their only trace was a rainbow straddling the valley and bright jewels of water shining on the grass around me. It was going to be a fabulous day.'

I ate a banana in bed, and enjoyed a splendid view for a meagre breakfast, before setting off in search of a breakfast more befitting my new role as credit card cycle tourer. I was in the hunt for coffee, bacon, and probably a second cup of coffee.

The morning began with a fine climb out of Buckden to loosen the limbs and shake the sleep from my eyes. It had me out of the saddle and working hard. I enjoyed imagining the speed at which professional cyclists could ride up here at. I wondered whether it would tire them at all. It certainly hurt me. But it also woke me up, ready for the hurtling descent down the other side. I tucked and accelerated wildly before chickening out, relaxing and sitting up, and enjoying the cruise down towards breakfast.

Outside Hawes, on a peaceful bend of a slow-moving river, was a wreath of remembrance to a soldier. The day's toughest climb followed soon after. I was propelled up Buttertubs Pass by the words of one of my favourite quatrains, written on the memorial wreath:

'We are the Pilgrims, master; we shall go
Always a little further: it may be
Beyond that last blue mountain barred with snow,
Across that angry or that glimmering sea.'

I knew nothing about that soldier – the wreath held no name or dates or 'Love From' clues. But my respect for him, for his regiment, for the sentiment behind the poem, and for the disquieting tranquillity of the setting all rolled around my mind as I ground my way up that long pass.

I hurtled down the other side and through the long valley of Swaledale towards Leyburn. I paused only for an invigorating swim in a cool peaty pool on the Swale, then summoned a last dollop of energy for the steep climb over the grouse moors. The high grounds were pink with summer heather. My legs were weary now, but a cup of tea in Leyburn and a pause at a brewery in Masham both helped morale as I began to wilt.

And now all that stood between me and my yellow jersey was a mad dash into Harrogate. I rode through the cheering, glorious crowds of my imagination towards the finish of a fabulous microadventure. I didn't mind one bit how pitiful my final stats were or how few people were actually there to welcome me across the finish line: none at all.

HOW TO RIDE LE TOUR DE YORKSHIRE

You could do the 120-mile ride in one long day, like the pros. It would be a nice challenge. Or you could spread it out into two more leisurely days, as I did.

The route runs from Leeds to Harrogate – the long way round (Leeds–Harewood–Otley–Ilkley–Skipton–Kettlewell–Aysgarth–Hawes–Reeth–Leyburn–Ripon–Harrogate). You will ride through beautiful scenery and past plenty of pubs and tea shops...

Wherever you live in the UK you can comfortably do this ride over a weekend. If you catch an early train to Leeds on Saturday morning you'll be there in time for lunch. Make sure to check in advance whether you need to reserve a place on the train for your bike. From Leeds a steady 40- to 50-mile ride will get you up into the quiet valley between Skipton and Buckden. Each village along there has a pub or two so you can have your evening meal whenever your stomach demands it. And you will effortlessly find a beautiful spot to sleep for the night.

In the morning the steep climb out of Buckden will build an appetite for breakfast in a cafe in Aysgarth or Bainbridge. Be sure to eat well because from Hawes you climb over Buttertubs, the biggest climb of the ride. There's a white-knuckle descent into the Muker valley and, apart from a whopper of a climb to reach Leyburn, you've now broken the back of the ride.

Pop into one of Masham's breweries for a quick morale-boosting sup and then it's an easy ride to Harrogate and the end. Take the train from Harrogate back to Leeds in time for your return train home.

HERE IS THE KIT I USED FOR THIS RIDE:

- Road bike.
- Helmet.
- I carried my kit on a seat post rack. You could also use panniers, a saddlebag or a small rucksack. (See page 214 for more advice on bikes.)
- I kept my gear in a 10-litre dry bag. A couple of bin bags would work fine for this. (See pages 210–11 for more advice on keeping your gear dry.)
- Multitool, pump, spare tube, puncture repair kit. Because you know what will happen if you gamble and don't take these things...
- Clothes: take only enough clothes so that, if you were soaking wet and wearing all of your clothes and pedalling, you would remain just about warm enough. If it gets any colder than that you can always head for a cafe or a train station! So for me, in August, this meant I only had the cycling clothes I was wearing. I took no spare clothes at all. I suppose I must have looked a bit of a geek sitting on the train up from London in my Lycra. At night I used all my clothes as a pillow.
- Buff. A concession to luxury – acted as a woolly hat, a sweatband or an eye patch.
- Tiny cycling rain jacket that packs down to smaller than a tennis ball.
- Bin bag: £ for lb this is the most effective, cheap, waterproof 'gilet' available and a great supplement to the tiny cycling rain jacket. Can also double as a make-do tarpaulin 'basha' above you at night if it rains. (See page 211 for more advice on building a basha.)
- Phone for camera and navigation. I used the phone on Airplane mode to save battery. Road map apps are available for smartphones that work even when you have no phone signal. (See page 230 for more advice on gadgetry.)
- Phone charger. A nice excuse to linger in a cafe for an hour whilst you charge your phone.

- Sleeping bag. The smallest one you own that will keep you more or less warm enough. (See page 207 for more advice.)
- Bivvy bag. (See pages 204–6 for more advice on bivvy bags.)
- Sleeping mat. Many experiments in not bothering with one have always led to me regretting leaving it behind. I used a Therm-a-Rest NeoAir ³/₄ length one. (See page 208 for more advice on sleeping mats.)
- Credit card.
- Toothbrush. Get a kiddy-size one. Or be gross, like me, and take chewing gum instead!

OTHER GREAT ROUTES TO RACE

I was fortunate, as a student, to run a mile on the Oxford University track at Iffley Road where Sir Roger Bannister broke the four-minute mile barrier. I have run many miles on many tracks, but the link to a great athletic endeavour made it far more enjoyable than usual. (Sir Roger, by the way, need not worry about me challenging his time.) In a similar vein, here are various routes of great races which would be fun to tackle at a more modest microadventure pace.

- Your local marathon route. Even if you are not a runner you could hike the route over a day, or cycle it in a couple of hours.
- Take on the 18th- and 19th-century challenges of 'walking wagers' or pedestrianism. Try to become a 'Centurion' by walking 100 miles in 24 hours. Or match Captain Barclay who walked 1,000 miles in 1,000 hours at Newmarket in 1809.
- The cycling route from the 2012 London Olympics. Alexander Vinoukorov covered the 155 miles in 5 hours 45 minutes, including nine laps of Box Hill.
- The Bob Graham Round is a cult classic, a challenge to cover 42 Lakeland fells in under 24 hours. Mere mortals would enjoy it as a fabulous 2-day hike.

16

WOODS AND FORESTS

Even small woods and forests feel removed from the world. They are almost a separate, parallel domain; like entering Narnia or Wonderland.

Time Required:	Overnight
Difficulty Level:	Low
Hassle Level:	Low
Essential Extra Kit:	As little as possible

When you enter a forest you step innocently across a threshold into a new world, one in which the normal rules of sound, light, weather and time do not apply. There is no horizon in a forest. There is no real view in a wood. The sensation is more like being underwater, immersed in a limpid green world. The air is quieter, darker and cooler. In a wood, rain takes longer to penetrate. So you can remain dry whilst those outside scurry for brollies. But the rain also continues to drip long after the sun returns. It may be less warm and less light than 'outside', but in the trees it can also be less cold and less windy. It is a more constant world in a wood. Though if you watch a wood over an entire year – running through it daily, for example – you notice the amazing changes from the dark, damp, vertically-striped monochrome world of winter, through the muffled marshmallow softness and roundness of summer woodland stuffed with foliage to the rustling russet shades of autumn.

My friends and I hadn't really planned much. There isn't a lot to report. We just stopped in a supermarket, loaded a basket with food and a bottle or two of cheap red wine and then headed out of town. Rain was falling, beating the river flat with a million tiny hammer taps of rain. We each carried a small backpack with the few things we needed for the night.

After 20 minutes of walking we were head-high in reeds. We could not see a single building. It is so easy to escape (from a town, from a computer, from a routine) if only you take the difficult step of making it happen. We didn't even mind the rain: if you've got the right gear, then rain need not dampen your spirits much. Besides, as angry little red-faced men in the army like to shout at you: 'if it ain't rainin', it ain't training!'

The rain fell on bluebells and pink dog's violet and cranesbill and the wood we entered was shining and wet. The warm, damp evening air brought out the strong smells of cow parsley beside the path. Birdsong and rain were the only sounds.

'From a lookout point we could still see the town we had left behind just a couple of miles ago and yet we were now in a dark green wood, damp with May rain, shining in the dusk light.'

We were not on our way to anywhere particularly beautiful or to do anything exciting: we just wanted to get away (or give ourselves the illusion of getting away) for a night. Sleeping in a wood is a perfect way of doing this. Jess told me that although she had lived around this town for all her life and that it was 'home', she had never done anything like this before. She sounded both surprised and pleased.

The UK is one of the least-wooded countries in Europe. You're only likely to be able to find small pockets of woodland around where you live, but the immersive nature of a wood means that you do not need much more than a small area. We reached the top of the woods. From a lookout point we could still see the town we had left behind just a couple of miles ago and yet we were now in a dark green wood, damp with May rain, shining in the dusk light. I love places like this. They illustrate the proximity of wildness, or even the proximity of an illusion of wildness. Though most of us live in a sanitised, suburbanised, *Subway*-ised world, we can still escape from it easily whenever we need to feel the rain blowing on our faces and howl at the moon.

Jess and Hannah set about lighting a small, careful fire, their hunger spurring them into action. Phil and I gathered firewood, grunting and heaving as we dragged huge lengths of wood far bigger than we ever intended to burn. Men seem to enjoy doing this.

We cooked a simple but delicious meal then stood around the fire chatting and laughing. It was only about 9pm but it felt far later. We toasted marshmallows (which, by the way, will taste better if they are not referred to as 'whales' nipples'), toasted the night with the last of the wine, and then slept.

In the morning the rain had stopped and the woods gleamed. Blackbirds and robins belted out the morning chorus. We felt grateful that we'd had the opportunity (or rather, that we had *created* the opportunity) to wake up in woodland with friends and the sound of birds singing.

'There's something about sleeping outside,' Hannah said, as we drank coffee, 'that feels really special. It's something that will stay with us. People might think we're mad but sometimes you've just got to do these things.'

FABULOUS FORESTS TO EXPLORE IN BRITAIN

- Glencoe's Woodland
- Forest of Dean
- New Forest
- Sherwood Forest
- Wistman's Wood

OTHER ENVIRONMENTS TO EXPLORE

- River
- Mountain
- Ocean
- Lake
- Desert: Dungeness is Britain's only desert.
- Underground: Great Douk Cave to Middle Washfold is an excellent first underground adventure. Search online for advice.
- Islands
- Urban

17

🔖 RIVER SWIM

I confess. I am a river geek. I love rivers. I look at rivers on maps and wonder how long they would take to navigate.

Time Required: .	1 Day +
Difficulty Level: .	Moderate
Location:	A River
Means of Transport:	Swim
Essential Extra Kit:	Dry bag, wetsuit, towel
Find Out More:	Watch the Video

I follow their thin blue line with my finger, tracing their path all the way up to the source, far away in the high lands, and down again all the way to the sea. When I cross a river in a car or train I crane my neck to snatch a quick downward glance: could I paddle or swim down there? Is it a good camping spot? Rivers are a superb starting point for hatching microadventure plans.

I have made many different types of journey, but I'd never done a swimming journey before. I'm not a strong swimmer so this was never going to be a long-distance expedition. I had never travelled so slowly and with such a low viewpoint on the world, but I was curious to find out what it would feel like to swim from Point A to Point B rather than just going back and forth in a swimming pool.

I borrowed a wetsuit and jumped in. The wetsuit was twenty years old, looked stupid, and was too thick and constricting for long-term swimming use. But part of the point of microadventures is to make do with what you have, rather than allowing expensive gear to become another barrier to entry. In fact, as I am not a very good swimmer, the thick wetsuit did not really inhibit my progress at all. My camping gear floated along behind me in a dry bag attached to a short length of rope.

I chose the River Thames for my swim. It's not a river associated with wildness and adventure. That is precisely why I chose it; because when you have a frog's-eye view the world suddenly becomes wild, wherever you may be. The perspective from which you look at the world dictates how it reflects back at you.

I felt I could be in any river in the world, so empty and remote did it feel. The water was warm, the sky was bright blue. At times I lay on my back and kicked my legs, my red waterproof bag drifting along gently behind me. I was having so much fun. I could not believe that I had never done a swimming journey before, even a tiny one like this. It was an experience quite unlike running or cycling or even canoeing. This most mundane and domesticated corner of southern England suddenly felt wild again.

I had begun in the picnic meadow of a small town. I swam past surprised grins and sun/booze-flushed faces in the riverside pub garden. I swam beneath a bridge and then I was into the wild. It was only Wiltshire, yes, but it was definitely wild. My eyes were but an inch or two above the water's surface and the river's banks towered above me, so I could see very little beyond the watery channel that was sweeping me gently along. The sun sweeping back and forth across the sky told me that my river was meandering through all points of the compass. It was disorientating and I found it impossible to gauge how fast I was travelling or which way I was heading. But it didn't matter. I was here to explore the river, so whichever way the river took me was the right way.

As I swam through a clump of bulrushes I startled red-beaked moorhens and a little brown reed warbler. I imagined shining pike lurking silently in the murky depths, waiting to nibble my toes. I kicked a little faster. I swam through lily pads, gently sweeping them aside with my hands as I glided by. I swam breaststroke, described by Roger Deakin, the patron saint of wild swimmers,

as 'the naturalist's stroke'. It is the best way to absorb all the sights and sensations. Besides, recent heavy rain meant that the warm water was thick with silt so there was nothing to see underwater. This was a pity as I had looked forward to exploring the utterly alien world beneath the surface. (I had originally toyed with snorkelling the entire journey in order to give an even more unusual perspective on a familiar place, but I couldn't find my snorkel.)

'I spent the night in that wood on the riverbank. I could not see lights or hear roads. I saw stars instead, peeping through the black mesh of branches and leaves above me.'

Down there in the Thames I could not see houses or the well-worn riverside footpath. Instead I saw birds on their nests, tucked inconspicuously against the riverbank. I passed them, peacefully. Perhaps we exchanged conspiratorial glances: I won't tell if you don't. I saw fish leap from the water. Cows grazing on the banks lumbered away in panic when they saw me. They had no idea what to make of me.

'In wild water you are on equal terms with the animal world around you; in every sense, on the same level,' wrote Roger Deakin, whose book, *Waterlog*, is essential reading for any fan of wild swimming. Swimming down a river for a couple of days was one of the most surprising experiences of all the microadventures I have tried.

After a long day of swimming and scrambling up and down the riverbank to film myself (one of my most ridiculous experiences of the always-ridiculous world of filming yourself doing stuff), I was very tired by sunset. I climbed out of the river into a copse of tall trees. I could hear only birdsong and the breeze among the branches. I draped my

soggy wetsuit in a tree to dry and pulled dry clothes from my pack. I sat down with my back to a tree and rested for a while. My muscles were aching. I had never swum so far in a day before. I caught myself nodding off to sleep and galvanised myself to cook some food before I slept.

I spent the night in that wood on the riverbank. I could not see lights or hear roads. I saw stars instead, peeping through the black mesh of branches and leaves above me. I listened to a long chorus of rooks. Throughout the night my little wood was alive with crashing beasts – deer, rabbits, foxes – and occasional fat fish leaped and splashed in the black river below.

The silent river slid by like a silver mirror. It was a magic carpet – step out into it and I would be carried to places new and adventures unimagined.'

I brewed coffee on a tiny fire of twigs at dawn. The silent river slid by like a silver mirror. It was a magic carpet – step out into it and I would be carried to places new and adventures unimagined.

But first, the two worst parts of the day:

1. Squeezing into my damp wetsuit.

2. The moment when the cold river, squeezing up inside the wetsuit, arrived at my crotch. There ought to be a word that specifically describes that sensation. I bet the Germans have one.

I eased myself down into the water (gasping and, yes, squealing a little) and began another day of swimming, wishing that I could carry on this journey all the way down to the sea and to its proper conclusion. It had been a revelation. Look at the normal with fresh eyes. Seek the extra-ordinary in the ordinary. Step away from the pleasant, unsurprising riverside picnic. Step away and slide down into the water. Be surprised. Swim a river.

WILD SWIMMING ADVICE

Wild swimming is fun, good for the soul and adventurous. But be careful about tides, currents, overhanging branches, unseen submerged obstacles and the cold. Be conservative in choosing where to swim, particularly when you are by yourself or at night (a full moon swim is a magical thing). However, as my definition of a wild swim is merely 'total submersion' (a rule laid down whilst trying to have a who-can-swim-in-the-most-rivers competition with a friend in wintertime Siberia), you don't have to be foolhardy or reckless. A mountain stream a foot deep and a foot wide can be perfect for a morning dip.

Safety aside, the most useful advice and encouragement I can offer if you are anxious about swimming in the wild is this:

You are not going to get eaten by a whale. Even when the water is cold, you never regret going for a bracing wild swim, you just perhaps dread it a little in advance. In this sense wild swimming is a cheesy-but-true metaphor for making yourself attempt difficult stuff in life: daunting in anticipation, tricky / nippy at first, not nearly as bad as you'd expected once you get going, and delightful, rewarding and uplifting once you have accomplished it. So tip-toe in and surprise yourself. Try to include a wild swim in every microadventure you do.

There are several excellent books filled with suggestions of places to wild swim. Search online for wild swimming and you'll find them as well as the useful Outdoor Swimming Society website.

OTHER RIVERS TO TRY

- ⊛ The Dart, Devon. Around New Bridge there are lots of swimming holes and bits you can snorkel or swim or tube down.
- ⊛ The Erme, Devon.
- ⊛ The Dwyfor, Gwynedd.
- ⊛ The Etive, Scottish Highlands.
- ⊛ The Wharfe, near Grassington, Yorkshire.
- ⊛ Symonds Yat Rock. An idyllic, peaceful look-out over the River Wye, woodland, fields, and the best of rural England.
- ⊛ Polldubh Falls on the River Nevis, Scottish Highlands. Try snorkelling beneath, it's 8m deep and full of tiny trout and sunlight glinting through the bubbles.
- ⊛ The Fairy Pools on Skye are magical – mountain-cold pools with water as clear as a swimming pool. Dive in from the rocks and swim beneath the underwater arch into the next pool.
- ⊛ An interesting challenge would be to 'swim up Snowdon', swimming the small lakes that are found as you ascend the mountain. Gone Swimming (www.goneswimming.co.uk) can organise this for you if you are not up for planning it yourself.
- ⊛ If you are in London or Cambridge, get involved with The Swimmer (www.theswimmer.org), a group who combine running across the city with swimming in all the outdoor pools and ponds.

19 SEA ADVENTURE

I paddled hard. The wave caught hold of the sea kayak and swept me up onto the beach. My friends, Simon and Rich, swooshed alongside.

Time Required:	Overnight
Location:	Anywhere on the coast
Difficulty Level:	Medium
Essential Extra Kit:	Sea kayak, fishing gear
Find Out More:	Watch the Video

We were the only people on the beach – the cliffs rising before us meant the only access to this strip of coastline was from the sea. We pulled the brightly-coloured boats up the empty swathe of sand, beyond the reach of the turquoise water. Not for the first time I was struck by how easy it is to find somewhere remote and surprising in Britain, if only you make a little effort to think originally and get off the beaten track.

Our plan had been simply to turn right at the mouth of the river and explore the coast. We would tow fishing lines behind us, hoping to catch something to cook that evening on a campfire on a deserted beach. We were not going far – it was more of a fun paddle to work up a bit of an appetite – but far enough to take us out

of the town to a deserted beach. Generating an illusion of remoteness and distance is almost as refreshing as the real thing. An important point of microadventures is not to feel duty-bound to overstretch yourself. If you have just a few hours before sunset do not feel you still have to attempt to travel to the ends of the earth. By the time we paddled out to sea it was late, and the water was perfectly flat, mirroring the blue sky above.

Sea kayaking puts a new perspective on familiar sights. Along a coastline busy with holidaymakers it allowed us to see things that mere landlubbers could not. We felt like explorers in an untravelled land as we steered into cool, dark sea caves. Back out in the bright sunshine, seals broached the calm surface close to our boats, snorting dismissively. When they dived I peered around excitedly, eager to spot where they would surface next. Guillemots flew swiftly overhead. But a dolphin trumped all the other wildlife when it leaped not far from us, to the accompaniment of three grown men's squeals of delight.

The kayaks cut smoothly through the clear water. The sea air smelled briskly fresh. We moved faster than walking speed for about the same amount of effort. Rich and Simon had already caught sea bass and mackerel on their lines. I was feeling competitive and envious. But, even though I am a novice fisherman, there was a mixture of relief and amazement when I felt a tug on my trailing line. I reeled in what can only be described as an absolutely enormous fish. I'd probably go so far as to say it was more like a whale than a fish… More truthful, perhaps, is the only statistic that really mattered: it was bigger than the others'.

The glassy sea slowly built to a gentle rolling swell. I enjoyed the feeling of speed on the waves' downhill slopes. The moon would be full this evening, so the tides were spring tides, larger than average. More than that, the moon was at perigee, the closest that it gets to Earth, which makes the tides even higher and the moon appear fatter and more impressive than ever. The technical name,

according to Wikipedia, is the 'perigee-syzygy of the Earth-Moon-Sun system'. The common term – 'supermoon' – is more fitting to how it looked later that night as it rose bright above the cove which sheltered us.

'The kayaks cut smoothly through the clear water. The sea air smelled briskly fresh. We moved faster than walking speed for about the same amount of effort.'

The spring tide also meant that we had little beach to aim for, as we were landing at the top of the tide. We pulled hard on the last few strokes and the boats ground to a halt on the sand. We climbed out onto a small scrap of beach. Above us green hills dotted with wind-sculpted pine trees rolled down before dropping off suddenly into the sheer cliff which sealed us onto the beach. We stretched and smiled.

A good thing about sea kayaking journeys is that you can carry plenty of kit. So now we donned wetsuits, masks and snorkels and swam out to some nearby rocks to try to supplement our fish supper. The rolling surf broke on the rocks, a beautiful milky green colour, and we held our breath and dived down amongst swirling kelp. We found mounds of spider crabs, their bodies as big as grapefruits, clinging to each other and the rocks. Spaniards will pay more for a spider crab than a lobster of the same weight, yet here we were able to simply reach down and pick up our dinner through no more effort than a refreshing evening swim.

We cooked our haul on a driftwood fire. There would be a hefty bill in a restaurant for that meal, but ours was free, with a view of the sun sinking over the sea thrown in. As night fell we piled a little more wood onto the fire. We sat round it sharing our favourite moments from the paddle and discussing the culturally difficult challenge of

'We felt like explorers in an untravelled land as we steered into cool, dark sea caves. Back out in the bright sunshine, seals broached the calm surface close to our boats, snorting dismissively.'

I wanted to get back to basics. To simplify my life; to get away from it all; to slow down for a bit. I got in touch with Nick, a friend I first met when he lived in a treehouse.

Time Required:	Up to you
Difficulty Level:	Medium
Location:	Up to you
Means of Transport:	None
Essential Extra Kit:	None
Find Out More:	Watch the Video

We decided to spend a few days in the woods together, living as simply as we could manage, and attempt to live solely off the land. We wanted to see whether we could have coped in the ancient days of hunter-gathering. The last song I heard before walking out into those green, fresh Sussex woods was Johnny Cash's rendition of 'Hurt'. It seemed prescient.

Off we went, equipped only with a knife, an axe and a bow-drill. We had some pre-made biltong and a haunch of meat from Nick's foraging school to start us off, for even cavemen would have had a small reserve store of supplies. As nicking birds' eggs is illegal, we took a box of eggs with us too. Whenever we found a wild nest we would allow ourselves one of our hens' eggs. We wore the clothes we stood up in and, like true Neanderthals, carried just a couple of furs for warmth at night. That was all. It was an easy trip to pack for.

Had I been alone, I would have lasted about an hour before boredom and hunger overcame me. But Nick is far more relaxed and patient than me, and he also has a fabulous level of knowledge about the natural world around us that lies unseen to virtually all of us. So we persevered. (I suppose for normal people, like you and me, the realistic alternative for this microadventure would be to pack a frugal amount of food, a few tea bags and a box of matches. Leave the smartphone behind. Head out alone into the woods for a while and attempt to still your racing mind.)

It was May, so we were too late for spring greens, too early for nuts and fruit. We lived on burdock roots, hop shoots, pig nuts and three-cornered leeks. These things are neither filling, nor particularly tasty, so we grew hungry. Very hungry. In between forays to find food we lit a fire with a bow-drill (by 'we' I mean 'Nick'). We built shelters from pliant hazel and hornbeam boughs and shivered, cold and hungry, through the night. We woke in the morning and spent the whole day searching for food again. And so the days passed. But it doesn't have to be fun to be fun...

Considering that we didn't go anywhere, didn't see much, and didn't really do much, this was a fascinating and memorable microadventure. Living in a 15-acre wood with no contact with the real world for a few days, and with all our meals, comfort and shelter entirely dependent on our hard work, was a difficult, enlightening and calming experience.

Back in London, heading home on the Underground, I noticed that nobody sat beside me in the carriage – I was grubby and I stank of wood smoke. My senses were alert after days in a quiet green world of wind and birdsong. I looked with more attention and interest at the everyday parts of life. Food smelled better. Women looked more beautiful. Music sounded richer. I made the most of the extra arm room to jot a few notes in my diary:

'With some thought, I figure it's Wednesday. I have to check the calendar on my phone for the date because I emerged only a couple of hours ago from the woods on this late spring evening. I was not far from home, but I feel I have been far from the world. Here is what I learned:

A bit of knowledge and a lot of practice pays off: Nick made fire from rubbing sticks together in just minutes. It was a magical sight.

Once you've lit a fire, gathered wood and built a shelter, it's quite boring for a buzzing mind to face the prospect of several days in a small wood with nothing to look forward to except the next inadequate meal.

To these things I am addicted: knowing the time, coffee, music, email, Twitter.

Food tastes better when you've earned it.

Wildness and beauty is never far away: you just have to seek it out.

'We decided to spend a few days in the woods together, living as simply as we could manage, and attempt to live solely off the land.'

Waking in the open air beside the embers of a smouldering fire to the sound of birdsong and the sight of the sun rising is good for the soul.

After a few hours of hating this stupid experiment, I noticed that my mind was slowing down. I was adjusting to having no phone, no internet, no news. Instead, I began to observe and really take note. I started looking hard for those tiny edible leaves; pausing at the rustling of rabbits; paying attention

to all the nature, red in tooth and claw, that was trying to survive alongside us in that wood.

My fingernails are still grubby. It feels too hot to be indoors. But the coffee tastes so snappy now, *O Soave Fanciulla* sounds so sweet, and my bed will feel wonderful as I fall asleep, grateful for the day's big lessons: simplify, slow down, focus only on the things that matter, and remember to be grateful.

TRY THIS FOR YOURSELF

If you would like to learn some bushcraft and foraging skills, try one of these courses:

England Sussex: Nick Weston, who I did this microadventure with, runs www.huntergathercook.com
Devon: www.wildfoodwalks.co.uk
Kent: www.fergustheforager.co.uk
Yorkshire: www.tastethewild.co.uk
Wales Pembrokeshire: www.llysmeddyg.com/short-breaks-pembrokeshire/short-courses-llys-meddyg/foraging
Scotland www.gallowaywildfoods.com www.wildwoodbushcraft.com/bushcraft_course_list_scotland.htm

21 CLOSE YOUR EYES. GO!

Time Required:	Up to you
Difficulty Level:	Medium
Location:	Up to you
Means of Transport:	Foot or bicycle
Essential Extra Kit:	Map, compass, and the skills to use them
Find Out More:	Watch the Video

In the years I spent travelling round the world I learned that the real highlights of travel are not the famous tourist hotspots. The best bits are the small, unexpected things you discover in the places in between. Machu Picchu was nice, but it wasn't a patch on riding the crazy mountain roads to get there. The pyramids are pleasant, but not as fun as cycling across the Sinai Peninsula to reach them. And so it goes on.

The world is a strange and wonderful place of infinite variety. What a shame then to only see sights you've already seen on TV. Be bold and brave and take a punt on a place that you know nothing about.

The same applies with microadventures. As much as possible I have tried to fill this book with ideas you can try anywhere, not tied to specific destinations and instructions. Microadventures are about making the most of your time and your surroundings rather than being limited by them.

Which is to say that all you need to do is grab a map, close your eyes, wave your finger above the map, then jab down randomly. You have now selected the objective for an interesting microadventure.

The aim is to travel, however you wish, to that randomly chosen point. The stuff you encounter, the things you see, the thoughts you think along the way: these will probably be more interesting than the random point on the map. But without having that destination to aim for in the first place, you are unlikely to do the hardest part of any adventure: begin.

You could try this idea with a map of your home town, with an Ordnance Survey map or, if you've really got guts and time to spare, with a map of the world! Spin the globe, adventurous stranger, and see where your destiny lies...

It is not quite cheating, but this idea certainly has more chance of a scenic outcome if you try it in the highlands of Scotland, as I did. I was eating a bacon butty in the cafe in Torridon, one of my favourite spots in Britain. My first jab of the finger landed mid-ocean. I poked again. I brushed the crumbs from my map and peered down at where I had pointed.

My finger had landed in the mountains. Red contour lines lay thick and jumbled, like a bowl of spaghetti. I tried to visualise how the ground would look from the contours and symbols on the map. Huddled into this tight corrie, halfway up the flank of a mountain massif, was a tiny circular loch. It looked as though I was going for a swim.

It was a grey morning and rain lashed against the windows. As usual I ordered one more cup of coffee. For the road. Before I go. I ran out of things to procrastinate about... The cafe was quiet and I was the only customer. Perhaps I imagined it, but I felt the waitress's eyes boring into my back, a look of scorn on her face. I sighed, paid, and walked out into the rain.

I headed out of town, chuntering to myself about what an idiot I was and doing my best to persuade myself that the sensible thing to do was return

to the cafe for a piece of cake. But once you are soaking wet you might as well accept it. You realise that things are not going to get any wetter. And in a little while you come to realise that you are not nearly as miserable as you are trying to pretend to yourself.

'The world is a strange and wonderful place of infinite variety. Be bold and brave and take a punt on a place that you know nothing about.'

The clouds lifted just enough to reveal the mountain tops around me. It really is a stunning part of the country and I began to enjoy trudging through the rain. The fact that I was not heading to any place in particular actually made me enjoy it more. My natural inclination is always to rush, to get where I am going as quickly as I can, but on this trip I had nothing much to do except savour the small moments along the way. So I detoured to climb a hill by scrambling up a boulder field rather than just trudging up the wet grass slope. It was a longer route, but it was more fun. One of the hills grew so steep that I had to resort to rock climbing for the final yards. It was difficult and frightening, for I am no climber. If I had fallen the consequences would have been unpleasant.

I slept high that night – sometimes it's the only way to escape the midges in Scotland. I was alone, high on a rainy Munro (a Scottish mountain higher than 3,000 feet). There was no view and I hadn't brought a book. It began to drizzle. It was neither particularly exciting nor particularly enjoyable, so I went to bed very early and dozed my way through a damp night.

Rainy nights in a bivvy are not great. You can do nothing except slide deeper into the bag, haul the hood up over your head and wait for morning. But whilst you may be less comfortable than in a

Travelodge, the reward is the deep draught of joy that comes from feeling completely free. Better this than the stifling hot sterility of a hotel room. In my normal life morning comes crashing in, sudden and unwelcome, with the awful beep of an alarm clock. Every morning begins with a brief register of regret. I wish it wasn't morning. I wish this day had not yet arrived. Psychologically, this cannot be a good start! But up there on my mountain, I was happy to wake up. The rain had stopped, the sky was clear and the view was sensational. I felt that I was a lucky man – luckier than a man with a damp sleeping bag and soggy crisps for breakfast ought to feel.

Anyone who has woken in the countryside knows how pleasant it is to walk outside and gaze up at the hills. On a clear morning, wet from rain, the air is sweet and fresh. Now imagine how much better that feels when you are up on top of those hills, when you feel as though all this is briefly yours...

I sat for a while on a boulder in the clear morning air and drank in the view. I was thrilled to be up there. The advantage of climbing a hill in the mist is the sensation of surprise if the weather improves like this and suddenly you see the world clear and vast beneath you for the first time. The drop beneath me was so steep that it looked more like the view from an aeroplane than from a mountain. I looked down the valley towards the grey sea loch. I could see the road I had trudged up yesterday morning in the rain. I was glad I had made the effort. A river ran beside it, sinewy and silver and the valley floor was flat until it climbed, abruptly, up the flanks of the craggy mountains, in a regular series of steep cliffs and brief ledges. The silence was absolute and, once I noticed it draped like a silk sheet across the land, I felt awkward to move and break it.

Perhaps this was the most pointless journey I had ever done. I was hiking to an arbitrary point on a map knowing full well that there was nothing there. All I would do once I arrived was turn around and return. But to dismiss this is to dismiss the entire genres of mountaineering and polar

'The clouds lifted just enough to reveal the mountain tops around me. It really is a stunning part of the country and I began to enjoy trudging through the rain. The fact that I was not heading to any place in particular actually made me enjoy it more.'

would have been impressive had I been able to see anything, but instead all I could see was the flat line of the water amongst the rocks and grass.

I smiled wryly to myself, removed my rucksack and sat down by the water. This was a place I would never have been to without this arbitrary exercise. In the interest of fairness I should also point out that this was a scene I probably wouldn't have missed never visiting, but that is the chance you have to take.

I sat and enjoyed the peace for as long as my impatient nature could bear. If I achieve nothing else from all these microadventures I hope that I can learn to sit still for a little while. The only way I could think to mark my arrival was to go for a swim. I stripped off, waded into the cold loch and swam out as far as I dared. I swam until I couldn't see the shore anymore. All I could see, whichever way I turned, was water and mist. It felt as though I was disappearing off the planet. I lost my nerve and turned back, back to my clothes and a jog down to the village for a well-earned cup of tea and that piece of cake.

adventure, not to mention leaving home to cycle all the way round the world simply to arrive back home again...

So I scrambled down and up rocky slopes, my legs wet from sweeping through heather and lank moorland grass. The weather closed in again. The clouds dropped until I was walking through the cold damp heart of one and unable to see much in front of me. I followed a compass bearing. I jumped small streams and balanced over rocks across the top of a waterfall. It would have been beautiful and inviting on a warm summer's day, but this is the lottery of adventuring in Britain: if you wait for a guarantee of fine weather you'll rarely go anywhere.

In a couple more hours I arrived at my grid reference. From my map I knew that rock walls rose sharply from three sides of the small loch. It

OTHER IDEAS LIKE THIS

Other ways to add the spice of randomness to your journeys include:

- ➡ Rolling a dice to decide your plans: 1= bike, 2= walk, 3= run, 4= swim, 5= canoe, 6= you decide.
- ➡ Spin a bottle when you reach junctions in the path to determine which direction to turn.
- ➡ Travel, as best as you can, directly along a compass bearing of your choice or a line of longitude.
- ➡ Geocaching is a fun activity for children and a good way of getting out on arbitrary journeys to places you have never been. Search online to learn more and find caches near to your home (see page 21).

ISLAND CAMP

As a boy I loved adventurous stories such as Enid Blyton's *Famous Five*, Willard Price's 'Adventure' series and Arthur Ransome's *Swallows and Amazons*.

Time Required:	Overnight
Difficulty Level:	Medium
Means of Transport:	Swimming
Essential Extra Kit:	Bin bags, warm clothes

I envied their adventures: sailing dinghies to explore small islands sounded like paradise.

Here's the thing: now that I am a grown-up it *still* sounds like paradise. Perhaps this means that I haven't really grown up, or perhaps being 'grown up' does not mean that our yearning for adventure and wilderness abates. Maybe it is actually *adults* – short of time, short of patience, full of ambition, full of frustration – who can really benefit from this sort of stuff.

Inspired by the spirit of *Swallows and Amazons*, my friends Alan, Ferg and I decided to sleep on an island for a night. We didn't have a sailing boat (nor any ginger beer) but that seemed a mere minor detail. To keep the equipment and logistics as simple as possible, and to maximise the challenge, we decided that we would swim to our island. The island was only about 100 metres off shore, which would have been an easy swim, had it not been very, very cold...

We stood on the lake shore, swaddled in woolly hats and down jackets. I questioned why I wanted to spend Valentine's Day getting near-naked in the freezing cold with other men. But whenever you think, 'this is an exciting idea' and immediately follow that by thinking, 'this is a very *stupid* idea' then you know you are on to a good thing and that you will regret it if you wimp out.

So we stripped off and we swam. 'Better drowned than duffers', after all.

We squealed. (At least, I squealed. Alan and Ferg were more stoic.) The water was extraordinarily cold. We made it. We shivered. We smiled. We lit a fire and warmed up.

Camping on an island feels unusual. It certainly feels different and more adventurous than being 'on land'. We cooked meat and drank wine. Alan, responsible for our supplies, had brought nothing but meat and wine. He argued, with good grounds, that you don't really need anything else for a good night. We chatted and laughed.

I enjoyed this microadventure very much. It was so simple, so cheap, so un-time-consuming, but it felt so important to hit the 'refresh and restart' button on our busy lives. That short swim across 100 metres of water removed us from the worries of the outside world. Stepping back from life, if only for one night, offers perspective and focus.

We lay in our bivvy bags, looking up at the stars through the gently swaying trees until we fell asleep. In the morning we cooked bacon and brewed coffee on the fire. We all felt nervous about having to repeat the swim back to shore. It was brutal, but it was also a very effective way of waking up. This time all three of us squealed.

I urge you to give something like this a go. The worst thing that can happen is that you hate it and decide that actually you love your normal life and a warm, comfy bed more than you had realised, and that's not a bad conclusion to reach. But I think it is more likely that you will treasure the microadventure *as well as* getting a better perspective on your normal life, the 'real world' that lies off your island and across the cold, clear lake... 'Grab a chance and you won't be sorry for a might-have-been.'

SOME ISLANDS I WOULD LOVE TO EXPLORE, THOUGH NOT NECESSARILY BY SWIMMING...

- ➲ The small islands off the coast of Wales such as Caldey, Ramsey, Skokholm, Skomer.
- ➲ The flat marsh islands of Essex like Skipper's, Horsey and Osea.
- ➲ Samson Island in the Scilly Isles.

See pages 153–6 for other ideas of microadventures inspired by books.

A JOURNEY FROM SOURCE TO SEA

Perhaps the greatest accessory to a microadventure is a river. Having boldly written that, I wonder whether actually it might be a hill. Or a bicycle. Or a bivvy bag...

Time Required:	Up to you
Difficulty Level:	Medium
Location:	Up to you
Means of Transport:	Something that floats
Find Out More:	Watch the Video

Anyway, a river is right up there near the top somewhere! There are more than 7,000 rivers to explore in Britain – which means more weekend outings than you have weekends left to live. And that's assuming you can travel the length of your river in just a weekend. You'd struggle with the Severn, Britain's longest river, which rises on the slopes of Plynlimon (a hill allegedly inhabited by a giant) before flowing for 220 miles down to the Severn Estuary. But even discounting the longest rivers, there are still thousands to explore.

I'm a long-term lover of rivers. I grew up building dams with my brother and our friends, jumping across streams and catching slippery little fish by hand. Later, as my eyes lifted to the horizon and I began taking journeys, I felt a stronger affinity with rivers than just as places to play. For each river is on a journey of its own, moving steadily from its beginning towards its end. This constant motion continues 24 hours a day, seven days a week for hundreds, thousands, maybe even millions of years.

Follow any river, any river on Earth, from its source down to the sea and you will find an interesting journey. You will encounter high lands and low lands and everything in between. Plus, your adventure will end at the sea, which is always a fine place to finish. And you will see a complete cross-section of landscape and society along the way.

Humans have always clustered round rivers. Many towns began strategically where a bend in a river offered a crook of protection or a site for a bridge. Others grew where the water was sweet, or where the banks splayed broad enough to be forded. The human aspect of rivers is interesting, so I would urge you to follow any river close to where you live, regardless of how tame the idea might sound initially.

But there is also something special about an unblemished, untamed river. I found myself in Scotland with a couple of days to spare and a packraft in the boot of my car, so I picked up a map

and looked for a river I could travel in just two days. I was spoiled for choice. I chose one, more or less at random, parked the car, shouldered my pack and headed up into the hills to walk to the source of my river. Foolishly, I forgot the map. But I did not worry much: all I had to do was follow a compass bearing for a day or so until I reached the river, then follow it down to the sea.

Getting to the start of the river was fun in itself. I tramped over nameless hills and through thick pine plantations. A herd of deer watched me, alert and quivering, then bolted when I made a sudden movement leaping over a stream. I slept on a bed of springy heather, almost certainly the only man out there on mile after mile of empty hills. I felt like a king, the proud owner of all I surveyed. This may in fact be the cheapest way to feel like a

millionaire (albeit a millionaire in a bivvy bag eating a squashed pork pie and being eaten by midges).

The next day I reached a tiny loch nestled near the summit of a hill. It was a lovely little spot, though unlikely to have a name or to feature in guidebooks. I would never have come here if I had not concocted this little trip.

I followed the stream that flowed from the loch, munching peanuts as I walked. It bounced steeply down through a copse of stunted, lichen-covered alder trees and over a series of small waterfalls. I picked my way alongside the stream. The weather was warm and dry. I hadn't seen a soul since leaving the road yesterday. I didn't care which direction I was heading in or what the terrain was like: I was following this little stream, wherever it took me, all the way to its journey's end at the sea. I liked how simple it was out here and how that allowed me to switch off from my thoughts and worries.

Hard work in the hills is a good thing, but my substantial lazy side was welcoming each stream and tributary that joined 'my' river and increased its size. I had walked a long way by now and each time the river grew took me closer to the moment when I could stop walking and take to the water instead. I inflated my little boat and, with a merry grin, began floating downstream. If I ever get to heaven I hope that there will be swift streams to paddle. (If you don't have a packraft you can still pick a suitably gentle river and use a rubber dinghy or even a tractor inner tube or lilo – see pages 127–31.)

The water was tinted the colour of whisky by the peat it had flowed across. I swept down small rapids and drifted above salmon on the slow, sinuous bends. I ducked beneath overhanging tree branches and hauled the raft over gravel flats when it was too shallow to paddle. Because the river was small, remote and not famous, I had all this entirely to myself. An hour or so before nightfall I was paddling the final lower reaches. The river was wide and slow, salmon rose for flies in each still pool and a heron watched me from the bank. At last the view ahead of me opened out. I had reached the sea! The excitement I felt was disproportionate to a two-day trip, but travelling from the source to the sea was such a satisfyingly complete journey that I felt delighted.

It was only after I packed away my boat at dusk on the deserted shingle beach and began the trek to the nearest railway station that I realised my mistake. I was not where I thought I was. I had not actually paddled the river that I had intended! I had ended up in a completely different bay to the one I anticipated reaching.

But this navigational error did not diminish my adventure – my competence, perhaps, but not the adventure. If anything, it served to confirm that it really does not matter where you go or what river you journey down. All that matters is that you paddle a river and seek adventure. There is no such thing as the wrong river...

USING BRITAIN'S RIVERS AND CANALS

As with everything else in this book, common sense and courtesy are key to paddling on Britain's waterways. Combining the two means that I have never had a problem or run into any arguments on a British river, despite the theoretical complications and legal grey areas over river access. In the unlikely event that problems arise, I suggest you follow the advice in the BCU handbook to English White Water: 'If you are challenged, behave reasonably and politely and leave as requested; that is usually the end of the matter.'

In general, Scotland has the best rights of access for paddlers in Britain, as they do for most outdoor activities. The Scottish Outdoor Access Code is integral to that. In England and Wales make sure you access a river via public land or ask permission if you need to cross private land. Be respectful of other river users, don't disrupt what anyone else is doing and be aware of issues such as birds' nesting seasons and salmon spawning beds.

Canoeing on river and canal navigations sometimes requires a licence, though some of the larger navigable non-tidal rivers can be paddled without one. The British Canoe Union is the governing body for canoeing and kayaking. Search online for up-to-date information about licences and the access code for waterways.

IF YOU LIKE THIS, YOU COULD ALSO TRY

- Any of the rivers on Dartmoor (such as the Dart, Erme, Plym or Okement) would make a good challenge because they rise in a featureless boggy plateau in the middle of the moor then head off in different directions.
- The Esk rises high on the flanks of Scafell Pike and races quickly down to the sea.
- The Leven drains out of Lake Windermere, only about eight miles from the sea.

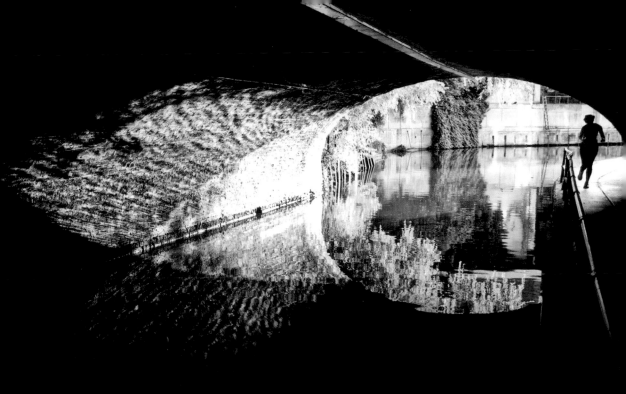

CANAL JOURNEY

As well as the rivers, do not neglect the 2,000 miles of canals around the UK, many of which can be enjoyed by the public.

Time Required:	Up to you
Difficulty Level:	Medium
Location:	Up to you
Means of Transport:	Something that floats
Essential Extra Kit:	Permit

Canals are an integral part of Britain's history and played a key role in the Industrial Revolution. They meander peacefully through much of Britain's less rural parts, acting as an oasis of calm and an avenue for microadventure for people living in built-up areas. But do not underestimate a canal's capacity for offering up a hard physical challenge.

Consider, for example, the 125-mile Devizes to Westminster canoe race, 'the longest non-stop canoe marathon in the world', in which the first 52 miles are on the Kennet and Avon Canal. The race takes place each year over the Easter weekend. It originally began, like many daft but life-affirming things, with a bet in a pub. It's a fantastic challenge and one I definitely recommend.

At the start line we feared we would not be allowed to begin. Everyone looked very professional and we had been told that at least four months of hard training were needed prior to the race. My friend Lucy and I had done two outings together before work. I had picked her as a partner because her mum's garden backed onto a river and we could keep our borrowed canoe there. I certainly did not pick her for butch, strong, canoeing shoulders. Then again, she'd probably say the same about me! But we were keen to give the race our best shot. The weather conditions were terrible and all the pre-race chatter left me feeling nervous, 'Hypothermia... snow... floods... worst ever conditions... very dangerous... months of training...'

accustomed to being squashed into a kayak, but they quickly began to lose their appeal.

The boat was shiny with ice and the night was long. But it was a beautiful experience too, and the memories of paddling quietly through towns at midnight are good ones. Music blared out of nightclubs ('nothing's gonna stop us now...'), the TV in a pub window showed someone running up to bowl in a cricket match, and well-lit trains thundered past as we crept slowly through the moonlit, frosty night.

By dawn we reached the River Thames, tired already and with 70-odd miles of river paddling still awaiting us. I had learned a lesson: do not underestimate our sleepy old canals...

'The boat was shiny with ice and the night was long. But it was a beautiful experience, too, and the memories of paddling quietly through towns at midnight are good ones.'

As we crossed the start line a marshall pointed out that my paddle was upside down. People were laughing at my stylish yellow washing-up gloves that I wore in place of proper canoeing ones. Our borrowed canoe was heavy and already leaking. But the sun was shining and things looked promising. The canal was beautiful and peaceful. However, soon the wind rose, night fell, snow began blowing horizontally into our faces and 125 miles started to sound like rather a long paddle.

We paddled through the night, beneath a magnificent Paschal full moon. You have to lift your boat out of the water and portage it 77 times during the race to bypass locks, and this includes one carry that is a mile long. I enjoyed the first few as a chance to stretch my legs, which were not

BEAUTIFUL STRETCHES OF CANAL TO EXPLORE

- Pontcysyllte Aqueduct – possibly the only paddle in the UK that can bring on serious vertigo!
- The Caledonian Canal.
- The Leeds–Liverpool Canal (the area around Gargrave is particularly scenic).
- Birmingham to Alvechurch.
- The Hatton Lock Flight.
- The Monmouthshire and Brecon Canal.
- The Norfolk Broads – not your standard canals, but beautiful nonetheless.

The Devizes to Westminster race takes place every Easter weekend. Entries open 1 January on www.dwrace.org.uk.

26 AN IMPROMPTU ESCAPE FROM THE OFFICE

I am busy. That phrase is the curse of our time. We are all busy, of course, but it's regarded as a boast, a badge of honour to be busy.

Time Required:	Overnight
Difficulty Level:	Easy
Location:	Local
Means of Transport:	Bicycle
Find Out More:	Watch the Video

'I'm so busy! I've got 300 emails! Admire me!' Busy, busy, busy, all the bloody time. Being busy makes it difficult to find time for adventure, difficult to find time for ourselves and for some fallow time in the wilderness.

This is why busy people need microadventures, to prevent the benefits of adventure from being squeezed out by the very busy-ness which makes it all the more vital. I feel really strongly that adventure must not become a peripheral part of my life. It should not become a fun but occasional thing, like a game of tennis or a trip to a circus. No. Adventure is more important to me than that.

Yet, evangelist for adventure or not, I was still too busy right now. There were planes to catch and bills to pay, so I needed to make this microadventure a brief one, just a snatched escape from my desk.

England had turned away from the sun. Winter. The days short and cold, the people indoors or else swaddled in warm coats, hands in pockets, eyes down and hurrying homewards. This was not a time for heading out to reconnect with nature, but I turned off my computer at 3pm. Like many self-employed people I get obsessed with my work and find it hard to stop. Idiotic, I know, when the essence of my 'work' is seeking adventure and

encouraging people to re-adjust their work–life balance more in the direction of adventure and the great outdoors. Do as I say, people, don't do as I do!

Anyway, I turned off my computer early and headed out the door. I lifted my pack onto my back and turned the key in the lock. The handlebars felt cold as I wheeled my bike out onto the street. I pulled on gloves and a thick jacket. The sun was already low in the sky, and its faint illusion of warmth was fading already. It was going to be a long and cold night.

British town centres are so bland and uniform. It is only when you venture out of your town that you get anything original, anything different to every other high street in the country. I had spent too long orbiting gently around this familiar sphere. It can be hard to escape the gravitational pull of familiarity and routine. Too often I am like an electron, held in tight with all the others by the nucleus of normality and conformity. But, like an electron, if I manage to escape then I blast away fizzing with energy. It feels exciting, a release – almost naughty somehow – to be riding away from town in the winter setting sun. To be heading out with nothing more sensible to do than sleep on a beach for the night, down there on the marshes.

I headed east, out of town, past the mums on the school run and the bums on the beer run. Past the newsagents' and the chip shops, past the small industrial units and out into the marshes where the wind was a-blowing. I don't know this land beyond my town.

Cars rushed past me with pine tree air fresheners dangling from rear-view mirrors, their occupants cocooned and warm. It was cold but beautiful out here, buffeted by the wind amongst the real trees. The low sun illuminated the winter crops as they shook in the wind, each stalk picked out, beautifully backlit with a slim halo of sunlight. There was just the briefest of twilights and then the sun was gone and it was dark. The darkness felt colder still.

I arrived at the seashore, down on the low-lying land east of London. It is a nothing land, a

nowhere land, half land, half water, half sea, half estuary. Not town, not quite country. But the beach was sheltered and deep with pebbles and sea shells. It would make a comfortable bed for the night.

I sat with my legs dangling down the sea wall as I ate fish and chips and stared out across the estuary. Two men passed me, walking their dogs. The dogs leaped and snarled at me from the end of their leads. The men were friendlier. One was fat, a sweatshirt stretched taut across his round stomach. The other man was older, skinny, with leather skin, a tattooed neck and dangling earrings which twinkled prettily in the light from the gas refinery away to our left.

They stopped and asked me what I was doing. Sometimes it's easier not to explain. To not talk about the frustrating clash of ambition against a lack of time; of restlessness and taking yourself too seriously; of life racing past too fast, unfulfilled; of spending too long in the warm sterility of indoors and not enough time out in the rawness of a winter night. So instead I just said I was looking at the stars.

'It'll be smashing out here tonight', they told me, to my surprise. I'd assumed they would think me weird and walk away.

The sky was clear, they pointed out. Good for stars. They liked to come out night fishing down here when they could find the time. Out on the mudflats over there. They'd dig for worms, for bait, then stand and fish for hours, deep into the night. Just the two of them. Mates. They loved it out here.

'It's what mates do, right?'

I agreed.

'A few beers and a night's fishing. Magic.'

They understood why I wanted to be out here, after all.

They could look past the ugly lights of Canvey Island that smeared the sky orange across on the north bank of the Thames. They could look beyond the gas refinery, the strange stink of chemicals, and the planes circling overhead waiting their turn to land at London's unsleeping airports. And they liked it out here. So did I. They understood that I might want to sit here, cold and dark, eating

fish and chips on my own and looking up at the stars. And to my surprise, for people always surprise you if only you let them, these two tough blokes were filled with questions about the stars.

'The low sun illuminated the winter crops as they shook in the wind, each stalk picked out, beautifully backlit with a slim halo of sunlight.'

I don't know much, in truth, but I shared what I could. I showed them how to find North using the stars (see page 238). Orientating yourself by the stars feels like a real connection with wilderness and the natural world, even in that post-industrial, almost post-apocalyptic overflow of London. I could imagine Riddley Walker feeling at home out there.

'Do you see the Plough up there?' I asked, pointing. 'It looks a bit like a frying pan.' They followed the direction of my arm, intrigued, and soon made out the pattern I was describing.

'Well, follow the line of the front of the pan. Follow it up for about two 'pan lengths'. The next bright star you see is the North Star – Polaris.'

They seemed pleased.

'It's above the North Pole,' I said. 'I want to go there one day.'

They wished me a good night and walked off with their dogs yanking the ropes in their hands. They tilted back their heads to drain their beer cans and perhaps to glance once more at the stars above us. They tossed their empty cans onto the beach, then it was just me and the night and the marshes.

These were Dickens's marshes 150 years ago. In *Great Expectations* Pip says, 'Ours was the marsh country, down by the river, within, as the river wound, 20 miles of the sea.'

He described the same land I had cycled through this afternoon, 'the dark flat wilderness, intersected with dykes and mounds and gates, with scattered cattle feeding on it... the low leaden line of the river... and the distance savage lair from which the wind was rushing, the sea.'

This remote-sounding Kent of 150 years ago today lies just 20 minutes from central London as you race past these unlovely but atmospheric marshlands on the fast train to Paris. It is here that the 'hulks', the old prison ships, used to be moored. This was the type of prison from which Magwitch escaped to terrify poor Pip. I realised that thoughts of escaped convicts were not conducive to a peaceful night sleeping alone on a beach! So I lit a small fire on the shingle and the warmth and light hid me from my imagination and the night. I warmed my hands on the fire as the sparks whirled around.

In the morning the night was gone and the world was harmless again. I had planned to swim but the tide was so far out that I could barely even see the sea, let alone swim in it. In its place was just miles of mud that seemed to be half water and half sky, covered by a mesh of tiny channels that reflected the sky's greys and blues. The only sound was the distinct repeating call of the curlew.

I stuffed away my sleeping bag, picked up a couple of discarded beer cans, then cycled back to my home in time for a shower, breakfast and another day at my desk.

Go on! Do it! Try a midweek microadventure. Leave work a little early, if possible, cycle out into the countryside, and spend a night out under the stars. Watch the sun rise from the warmth of your sleeping bag, and then ride back to work. Slope back in a little late, if you can get away with that. You may get to work an hour late and a bit smelly, but I think that is a small price to pay. Midweek microadventures are so invigorating, so good for the soul that I am convinced you'll more than make up for those lost hours with better quality work once you return.

ADVICE ON STAYING WARM ON A WINTER BIVVY

- Stay low – for every 100 metres you climb up a hill the temperature drops by around 1° Celsius. But avoid valley floors too because cold air settles down there.
- Stay out of the wind – finding a secluded spot to sleep will keep you much warmer.
- Wear a woolly hat, even for sleeping.
- Don't sleep in wet clothes.
- Wear lots of loose layers.
- Get used to the 'hood' on sleeping bags and the claustrophobic feeling of pulling the draw-cord tight to leave just a small breathing hole.
- Eat well before going to bed. A hot, fatty meal takes a long time to digest and helps keeps you warm through the night.
- Go to bed warm. Your sleeping bag insulates you – it doesn't warm you. This may entail a burst of star jumps or press ups before getting into the sleeping bag, or doing sit-ups once you are inside it.
- If you have a camping stove then heat some water for a hot water bottle. Make sure the lid's on tight and it is not too hot.

WILDERNESS ADVENTURE

Time Required:	2 days +
Difficulty Level:	Quite hard
Location:	North-west Scotland
Means of Transport:	Foot
Essential Extra Kit:	All your food for the duration of your visit
Find Out More:	Watch the Video

The landscapes grew in beauty and scale. I had been driving north for hours but at last I reached the end of the road at Mallaig. I parked my hire car, always the fastest car on the road, and leaped aboard the little ferry with less than a minute to spare. It was time to slow down.

I was heading to the Knoydart peninsula for some proper wilderness. This book hopes to emphasise that even the *illusion* of wildness, those tiny forgotten pockets of it squeezed behind your town, can refresh the soul, but there is still something extra special about the *proper* wild places. Knoydart is famously isolated, at least by the standards of the overcrowded British mainland. The only way to reach it is by ferry or by walking across rugged open country for a day or two.

I had no particular reason for coming to Knoydart, I had not earmarked any particular challenge or specific mountains that I wanted to tackle. I simply wanted to feel a bit more cut-off than I usually do. Truth be told, when I climbed off the ferry I was at a bit of a loose end at first. I'm not very good at having no plans. I walked around the tiny hamlet of Inverie where the ferry docks. The

Up there I conceded defeat to the gales and the snow. I wasn't having fun. I decided to quit.

It's hard to explain the thought processes when deciding whether to persevere or to give up. The only certain thing is that the arguments used to come to a decision are very different before a trip, during a trip and after it. What seems important now may seem less so when looked back on later.

In the larger expeditions I have done I have skirted this conundrum in a simple, if pig-headed way: quitting has never been an option. End of discussion. Quitting is absolute anathema. I've flirted with the idea, certainly – I do that all the time! But I have never allowed myself to submit. I seem to have spent much of my life ploughing stubbornly forwards in the hope of one day gaining some sort of retrospective pleasure. It's known as Type 2 fun. All misery is acceptable – the theory goes – in the hope that, at some indeterminate point in an indeterminate future, I will look back at this moment and be glad I persevered.

long downpours of heavy rain. The only constant in the weather was the wind which rolled down from the mountains, strong and cold. The hills across the sea loch were silhouettes now, differentiated from each other only by their shades of grey.

The pub's business card declared that 'Walkers, trampers, dogs, kids, anarchists, musicians' were all welcome. There was a T-shirt for sale on the wall ('Up a mountain, down a beer') as well as a guitar, a violin and the head of a woolly sheep. The fireplace was built of huge, dark cubes of rock and topped with a gnarled, blackened log for a lintel. With glowing face and stinging eyes, I removed my boots and slid onto a chair. It felt so good to have wimped out of that miserable bloody mountain climb and to be sitting in the pub instead!

You could walk 50 miles from that pub without hitting a road. By British standards that is an extraordinary expanse of epic wilderness and definitely worth a visit, even if, like me, you do not achieve anything even vaguely epic along the way.

> 'I seem to have spent much of my life ploughing stubbornly forwards in the hope of one day gaining some sort of retrospective pleasure. It's known as Type 2 fun.'

Perhaps this is why giving up on this blustery, wet microadventure gave me a little extra burst of pleasure. In my big trip mentality I would have forced myself to stick it out up there, no matter how miserable the experience. This now made turning round and scampering down to the pub in Inverie all the sweeter! So I retreated, defeated but happy.

On a different microadventure I had visited Britain's most northerly pub (pages 167–75). Here, battered and wet, I sought refuge in 'the remotest pub in mainland Britain' – the Old Forge Inn. Out of the window the bay was shining now between

OTHER REMOTE AREAS TO EXPLORE

- ➲ Cape Wrath, Scottish Highlands.
- ➲ Loch Coruisk, Isle of Skye.
- ➲ Wasdale, Cumbria.
- ➲ Spurn Point, East Yorkshire.
- ➲ Grid reference NH02020 is apparently mainland Britain's most isolated spot, the furthest from any road.

BUILDING A WILD HUT

Time Required:	1 day
Difficulty Level:	Hard
Location:	Local
Essential Extra Kit:	Saw, string
Find Out More:	Watch the Video

Nothing beats an unexpected email from a stranger with a great idea. One of the best I've received was from Kevin in Glasgow. He invited me to help him build a wild hut from natural materials and then to sleep in it: 'If you're up for building an epic wild hut I'd love to hear from you.' Kevin is slowly working his way through building 100 different wild huts all over Scotland. I am hopeless at stuff like this but it sounded fun and so I said 'yes'.

Kevin organised all the logistics for this microadventure. So, as he pulled the bags from the boot of his car in a car park outside Perth I was pleased to see, amongst the saws and sleeping bags, a very large packet of sausages. There were four of us. Kevin had brought his friend Rich along to help and I had recruited my friend Mark. We had a lot of work ahead of us, so many hands would help things along. We began climbing the hill that

was to become our home for the night. It was mid-afternoon on a cold, grey March day and the only other people on the hill were dog walkers and a few ambling elderly people.

We passed the gruesome remains of a family of near-melted snowmen. The air was cold and patches of snow lay on the ground alongside a couple of children's dens. The pyramids of sticks were not very technical but must have been fun to build. A lot of the microadventures I have done have felt as though I was just playing. It took me some time to not worry about this, not to feel defensive or fear that I was wasting my time. Children play because it is fun and escapism, but also because they are learning and developing. These are good things for adults to do as well. We four overgrown boys were on our way to build a den of our own.

We emerged from the woods onto a high clifftop beside a crumbling tower. The view was spectacular: to our left, the River Tay flowed sedately towards the sea, while to our right lay the city of Perth. Directly below us was the motorway. I had taken a taxi along that motorway one Sunday morning a year before, hungover, heading home from a friend's wedding. I remember looking up at this steep hill, seeing the tower and thinking what a good hill it would be to climb one day.

Winter days are short in Scotland, so time was of the essence. We fanned out into the woods searching for suitable wood to build with. We did not want to damage trees so we only used dead, fallen wood. We gathered long, strong, slender branches – 10 foot long and as thick as our wrist were ideal – which would form the frame of the hut.

The plan was to construct four separate single beds with a three-sided pyramid roof above. We cut the branches to the right length and then tied them together with flimsy garden twine. This biodegradable twine was the only man-made material used in the structure; it was not very strong, but Kevin assured me that it was not supposed to provide any structural strength.

The twine would just hold the joints temporarily together until they were wedged tightly into place by other lengths of wood. Indeed, by the end of the project everything had meshed together so tightly that the hut was phenomenally sturdy.

With the roof's frame complete, we built the frames of the beds and laid small sticks across the top. Later we would make it more comfortable with armfuls of dry grass. The only mistake we made, which we discovered too late, was that once the roof was in place the beds were a little short.

Next we began to build the roof panels. It seemed an ambitious design. It was an interesting learning experience for me to build this hut with people who were more skilled, patient and imaginative than me. First we lashed together a triangular frame of branches and covered it with a lattice of sticks. We piled about 18 inches of bracken and dead leaves on top then squashed it together with another triangular frame. I think the technical name for this is a Cheese Toasty Roofing Panel. We repeated the process three times. Each panel was very heavy and required three men to lift into position.

'We began climbing the hill that was to become our home for the night. It was mid-afternoon on a cold, grey March day and the only other people on the hill were dog walkers and a few ambling elderly people.'

Rain began to fall. It threatened sleet, but we continued to work. Dusk arrived, swiftly, and the lights of towns began to shine through the gloom. The road beneath us was a mesmerising river of white and red lights. It looked beautiful from here but I was glad to be up on this hilltop, above those rush hour queues, and free for a little while.

I enjoy microadventures close to built-up areas as they confirm that you do not need to travel far from a town to find something new and different. As evening descended and people returned to their homes, we were out in the wild building a home of our own.

Rich began to light the fire. The flames brought colour and warmth and soon the smell of sausages filled the air. Standing around a fire, sharing warmth and light and food with interesting people: these are things I never tire of. We were close to a city but sufficiently distant to feel the cold of the snow and the rain. Whether we had a warm, comfortable night would depend completely upon our own hard work and skills. I liked that.

The hut took ten hours to build. We wouldn't even sleep in it for that long, but that was not really the point. The time had come to test it. We'd made our bed, so now we had to lie in it. We began the huffing and puffing wriggling process of climbing into sleeping bags in a homemade hut high on a hilltop. The beds were surprisingly sturdy and comfortable, so long as you avoided the occasional sharp stick jabbing into your back. There was much whinging and complaining and moaning about the beds being too small. Allegations abounded that I, the token Englishman, was the biggest complainer.

I disputed this vigorously, though suspected there may have been a grain of truth to the allegations. (But I definitely *did* get the shortest bed...) At least all the wriggling to get into a sleeping bag warmed us up. It was one of my most enjoyable sleeps of the year.

What did I get from this experience? I visited somewhere new. I met interesting people. I did something I've never done before. I learned new skills. And it was fun. (I try not to underestimate the importance of that.) It was also a good reminder that working hard and making something that you can be proud of is a satisfying accomplishment. Too often I am slapdash, hurried and impatient. I loved building this hut, spending time pottering around the woods, clearing my head, working hard, and escaping from life for a while.

OTHER THINGS TO TRY TO BUILD

- A coracle
- A pizza oven
- A writing shed
- A treehouse
- A birchbark canoe

29

A JOURNEY ON THE TUBE

GT Tyres in West Wales is not a hub of adventure. Indeed we were met, that afternoon, with something approaching good-humoured incredulity.

Time Required:	A few hours to a few days
Difficulty Level:	Medium
Location:	A river deep enough to float on
Means of Transport:	Tractor inner tube
Essential Extra Kit:	Paddle, dry bags
Find Out More:	Watch the Video

There was a huge pile of old tyres in one corner, jumbled all the way up to the ceiling. Paint was peeling from the walls and loose wires dangled from sockets. A sagging banner boasted that the Maxxis M-36 was The New Leading Edge Asymmetric. I had never been into a tyre shop before, I realised. Is that an admission that I'm not as manly as I ought to be?

The men working there laughed at our request to buy four tractor inner tubes, but cheerfully inflated them for us. £50 for four tubes is nicely at the bargain end of the scale of adventuring boats (think canoes, dinghies, yachts, Gordon Tracy submarines...). They thought we were daft, and I was amazed that they worked, surrounded by inner tubes, next to a river and yet had never set sail.

A family came down to the river bank to watch us launch. The kids stood silently and stared at us. We clambered aboard, waved at them as heroically

as it is possible to do from an inner tube, and pushed out into the current. A handy feature of river journeys is that you can take far more clobber than on a bicycle or on your back. We were towing our essential gear – camping gear, food, cast-iron cooking pot, booze – in dry bags but we did not know how well they would float until we began. We were relieved that they didn't sink.

It's exciting to head into the unknown: all the greatest adventures are marinated with the spice of uncertainty. The same applies on a quiet Wednesday afternoon on a gentle river in a small town in Wales. We drifted out of town. It took some time to get used to travelling so slowly. After about half an hour we could still see the spot we had launched from. There is a good rule for travel that the slower your journey, the richer the experience will be. We drifted slowly or paddled languidly,

sometimes together, sometimes in single file, or all apart and as lonely as a cloud.

The water was brown and murky. Thick green trees overhung the riverbanks. It almost felt like a journey down the Amazon. Almost. I looked around contentedly. Alex was paddling gently. Ruben was sitting back with his hands behind his head, the very picture of a man feeling rather chuffed to have left the office behind. Ade, who had opted to bring flippers rather than a paddle, was merrily kicking his legs, splashing like a toddler in the bath and steaming off ahead of the rest of us.

This journey was not quite Amazonian in scale as we had only a handful of miles to travel to reach the mouth of the river and the beach. After a few long bends the river began to widen. Mooring buoys bobbed in the gentle current. We passed

'It's exciting to head into the
unknown: all the greatest
adventures are marinated with
the spice of uncertainty.
The same applies on a quiet
Wednesday afternoon on a gentle
river in a small town in Wales.'

a small red boat – 'Searcher' – and a blue one on
which an old man was working.

'Now that's a cheap way to go boating', he called
out, in the vexed tones of boat-owning men who
spend more time and money on fixing their boats
than they do actually sailing them.

We passed a few houses, their gardens stretching
down to the river bank. I'd love to live beside a river.
I am reaching a stage in life where I find myself
envious of men with sheds. A blue shed overlooked
the river, the water reflecting in its windows. It was
a beauty. If only I lived here, I mused... If only I had
that man's shed... All my problems would be solved.
I would write great books in that shed. I would
swim in this river every day. I would be a better
person. More efficient. Content at last...

I have similar thoughts on almost every trip
I do. It was a cottage I was after on Knoydart, a

better bike in Strathpeffer, a farm in Devon, a cafe in Torridon and a gentle job as a postman on the Shetland Isles. But I know too that when I am away on big overseas expeditions I yearn for the home I already have; yearning for home and vowing that this time, this time, I will write great books and be a better, more efficient, more content man...

And, such is human nature, I realised that if the man in the shed had looked up from the manuscript of his great novel and seen four idiots floating past on tractor tubes, then *he* would probably have been jealous of *us* and wished himself out here on this adventure.

So I turned away from the shed and all that it may or may not represent and I looked forward instead, down the river. I loved floating downstream, lounging as comfortably as on a beanbag. The river and the view were opening

out now. On both sides were low hills, the fields green amid patches of yellow gorse. These hills formed the valley that was funnelling us now down towards the sea. The river mouth was broad and the tide was ebbing strongly. The flow was fast and we bobbed along merrily. Sand banks were appearing in the river as the water level dropped. Our course was now determined more by the whims of the current than by our own seamanship. Three of us went one way round a sandbar, one went another, but we were all sweeping, one way or another, around an enormous left-hand bend towards the sea. We were beneath a sea sky now, a sky larger than an ordinary one that has been nibbled into by trees and buildings and hills.

An eddy led us gently to the beach. The small fishing boats we had passed began to swing round on their moorings in the slack tide. The river was

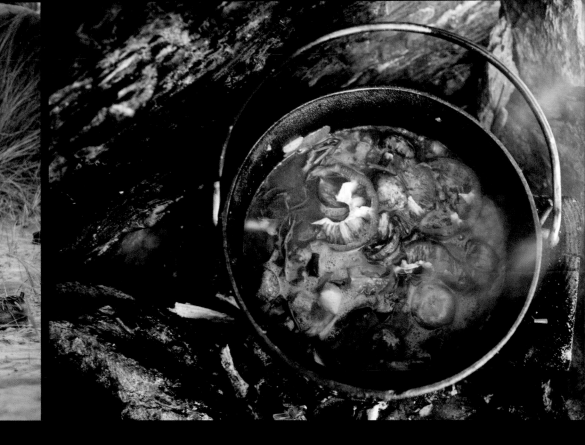

beginning to flow back up the way it had come. We had arrived just in time. We laughed and talked loudly, chuffed that the trip had worked so well and that we'd made it to the beach just in time.

The weather had turned a little too. The blue skies we had begun beneath had lowered and darkened to a more familiar Welsh grey. We carried our bags and the bulky inner tubes up the windy beach and found a sheltered spot we could camp in among the dunes, surrounded by gorse and the spiky green-brown dune grass fretting and fidgeting in the breeze.

We changed clothes then fanned out to gather firewood. We returned with armfuls of ocean-smoothed driftwood. Ruben, barefoot in jeans and a black hoody, began to build the fire that we would cook on. Alex returned last, and slowly. He was grinning like a man who knew he had found the biggest piece of firewood as he hauled a massive log up into the dunes.

The inner tubes transmogrified magically from fabulous water craft to fabulous armchairs. There was merriment and amusement all round. We dug out four enamel mugs, opened a bottle of wine (brought along for cookery reasons, of course) and toasted an epic river journey.

And, in case you think you need a tractor tube and a river to enjoy an evening like this with your friends, the next chapter is one that anyone can do, any time...

30

GOING OUT FOR DINNER

Midweek in the working week: the old 9-to-5 grind. Work, sleep, work, working slowly towards the weekend. But even sensible folk with proper jobs and respectable bedtimes squeeze some fun into the week.

Time Required:	Overnight
Difficulty Level:	Medium – a little advance planning is required
Location:	Local
Essential Extra Kit:	Good food, friends
Find Out More:	Watch the Video

Friends gather for dinner, at someone's home or a restaurant, or perhaps they go to a pub to enjoy a meal and talk rubbish together over a few drinks. If this is the sort of fun evening you enjoy then here is an idea for a sociable midweek microadventure.

A strange aspect of living in a big city, which took some time to get used to, is that if your friends live on the other side of town then going to see them can feel like a hassle. Throw in a combination of busy diaries and a bit of general male crapness towards bothering to keep in touch, and months can pass before my friends and I find ourselves all together. So we picked a date then travelled from four different places after work, convening in the small country pub at the end of the train line.

It was around 6.30 on a mild evening. We waited for the barman to notice that he was no longer alone. As we sat down, four fresh-pulled pints of local beer before us, there was a palpable sense of relaxation. We were excited. We felt the weight of the city lifting from our shoulders. The beers did not last long – first beers never do – and then we were outside, out of the village, and climbing a small hill. We were hungry.

'The day was seeping from the sky now as our dinner bubbled away on the fire. The boughs of a beech tree arched over our camp spot.'

Every time I escape from a city for the night, I am struck by how beautiful and peaceful the countryside is. I always vow to do it more often. But when I am in the city I find it hard to imagine that in any direction there lies, eventually, countryside and hilltops, cow parsley and cow pats, even cows. A city seems a difficult thing to escape from. It would feel more fitting, almost, if there was an actual boundary to cross, a clearly defined line that could only be crossed with some difficulty. On one side is the city, on the other is countryside – a foreign place where they do things differently. Perhaps it ought to be as difficult to cross as it feels, to take effort and paperwork, or at the very least to require proper equipment and carefully thought-through plans. In other words, when I am in the city it seems as though escaping ought to be more difficult than jumping on the 5.15pm train, meeting your mates for a quick pint, and then sauntering up a grassy slope in the same clothes I'd worn in meetings all day.

I had enjoyed those meetings all the more knowing that shortly I'd be getting out of town. I liked the minutes of small talk at the end when someone asks 'Got any plans for tonight?' and the mixed looks of amusement, astonishment, envy and - occasionally - whatever the opposite of envy is when I reply, 'Oh, I'm just meeting a few friends for a meal. On top of a hill.'

These looks confirm to me that the hint of gentle madness and subversiveness is one of the bits I like best about microadventures.

About two-thirds of the way up the hill we paused and turned around. Paragliders were curving and soaring above our heads, making the

most of the favourable early evening thermals. Down in the valley a train moved slowly along the track we had recently arrived on. The first oilseed rape fields were blooming, squares of dazzling yellow in the patchwork of green fields that stretched away as far as we could see. Amongst the fields were small villages and church spires. It was hard to imagine that somewhere, over there, lay a massive city.

We turned and climbed once more. We were in no hurry, chatting and laughing as we walked, but even so it was not long before we arrived at the small copse where we were going to spend the night. We gathered firewood into three piles: small dry twigs for kindling, sticks (mostly elder) to get the fire established, and then a pile of large logs to burn into the night. The fire was soon blazing happily. The sun had dropped behind the hill now, casting our little spot into shadow.

I reached into my pack and emptied out the contents. Normally food is quite low on my priorities for a night away. Depending on the circumstances, I either take basic camping food, eat something before I leave, or make do with sandwiches and a squashed pork pie. But tonight it was all about the food. And the fire. And the hilltop. And the beer. And the wine.

I pulled from my pack an old pan, battered and bent and blackened by previous campfires, then a handful of loose vegetables, a crusty loaf, only a little bit squashed and out of shape, some stewing steak, a bottle of red wine and, lastly, the crowning glory: an eight-pint flagon of ale.

One of the best things about a good stew is how simple it is to prepare. There really is not much to do other than chop everything into chunks, bung it into a pan with half a bottle of wine, and stick it on top of the fire. We poured ourselves another beer and sat down to wait. The longer you can bear to wait, the better the stew becomes.

The day was seeping from the sky now as our dinner bubbled away on the fire. The boughs of a beech tree arched over our camp spot. I reached up

and felt the sticky buds – the leaves were beginning to unfurl. The long, grey winter was almost behind us. The new leaves were pale green, thin and soft and delicate. Most of the branches above our heads were still bare. The black branches broke the sky into a mosaic of darkening blue. Each piece of mosaic shifted and changed slightly as a gentle breeze moved through the tree but each changing piece still fitted perfectly with the others.

The glow of the fire began to shine on our faces as dusk settled further. I spotted the first stars. Perhaps they had been out for a while, but only now was I sufficiently still and alert to notice them. Someone added more wood to the fire, stirred the stew, topped up our beer. The smoke from the fire moved round and engulfed me. My eyes smarted and I scrunched them up, waiting for the breath of breeze to pass and the smoke to move on. I love the smell of wood smoke. It reminds me of my dad's bonfires and of wild camps on hundreds of nights all across the world. The best times of my life. And I like the smell when it lingers on my clothes into the next morning. The sweet vagabond's perfume of freedom mingling with the commuters' aftershave and polystyrene coffees on the train back into town.

'The glow of the fire began to shine on our faces as dusk settled further. I spotted the first stars. Perhaps they had been out for a while, but only now was I sufficiently still and alert to notice them.'

Another beer. Another stir of the stew.

There was a late spring nip to the air and we piled the fire a little higher. We were lounging back against big logs, talking rubbish and sharing dreams. Einstein said that 'creativity is the residue only an hour from the city's restaurants but there was nowhere we'd rather have been than here.

We ate second helpings and wiped the pan and our bowls clean with the last of the bread. Then there was nothing to do but lie back beside the fire, chat and finish the wine and the beer.

It was not late, but because we live in an artificial world of electric lights our bodies tend to get confused by darkness. So we felt sleepy far earlier than if we were in a pub down there in the real world. We arranged our sleeping bags round the fire. There's nothing nicer than to wake in the middle of the night beside the soft warm glow of a bed of embers.

'The stew smelled so good now. It was bubbling full to the brim, rich and thick, boiling gently amidst the crackle of flames and the throbbing red embers.'

Curious sheep were watching us when I woke. They stood in a line a few metres away. There was not a cloud in the sky. It was a perfect, silent morning. The sheep stared blankly. I imagined them to be thinking, 'Who are you, Strange Things, lying in our field? We have mornings like this every

I imagine, who might read this book.

If it is you, why not try this sometime soon? Persuade your friends that the next time you all meet up you should do it on a hilltop. It's nothing particularly different – you'll spend time together, eat good food, drink and laugh together, and be back on your normal train into work the next morning. It's nothing particularly different, but it is so different that I bet you'll still be talking about it a year from now.

See page 221 for fire etiquette and pages 222-3 for campfire recipes.

This was likely to be my shortest, simplest night on a hill all year. I was on a family holiday in Cornwall. But I still wanted to be outdoors on the night of the Summer Solstice.

SUMMER SOLSTICE

SUNRISE:	4.43AM
SUNSET:	9.21PM
MOONRISE:	7.05PM
MOONSET:	2.58AM
MOON IS 96.3% FULL	

We were beside the seaside so the logistics of finding a peaceful bivvy spot were simple. I had my eye on a fine hill just 15 minutes' walk from the dinner table where we sat. The windows of the house were open, the weather was fine and warm. We had eaten well and the evening was winding down. The sun had already set. My wife, Sarah, decided that she would like to come along too. I quickly packed a small bag with everything we needed for the night, Sarah stuffed a couple of pillows into a wicker basket and off we went.

But all of a sudden the weather closed in. The infuriating British weather, so fickle that you can never predict how things will turn out. By that same account though, you can never let the weather dictate what you do. You'd never do anything outdoors in Britain if you waited for guaranteed fine weather. You have to take your chances. Sometimes you win. Sometimes you do not.

The first drops of rain fell.

We were not winning.

By the time we reached the shore it was raining steadily. It was a warm solstice rain but it was still a wet rain, falling from an increasingly dark sky. This was beginning to feel like quite a bad idea. Indeed, had it not been the Summer Solstice I would have returned to the house and saved it for another day.

But I love the solstice so I was keen to persevere. I offered various guilt-free get-out options to Sarah, giving her the chance to return home to a dry bed without too many accusations from me about being a wimp. But she remained adamant and we continued together.

Across the estuary a Take That tribute band were performing. Muffled slightly by the driving rain and the distance, we heard them singing that today this could be the greatest day of our lives.

This, I was forced to concede, seemed unlikely. It was pouring down. Bucketing down. Tipping down.

'*Pissing down*', was how Sarah described it, with feeling, hissing through clenched teeth.

We were on top of the hill now. It was dark and it was raining extraordinarily hard. I shoved our sleeping bags into bivvy bags as fast as I could whilst maintaining an almost maniacal enthusiasm.

'Isn't this fun?' I called enthusiastically through the torrential cold rain, knowing very well that it was not. 'Woo hoo!'

We climbed into our sleeping bags in a small dip just off the summit of the hill. We were sheltered, at least, from the wind. We didn't speak. There was not a lot to say. I was tempted to reinforce my 'Isn't-this-fun-woo-hoo!' refrain but I thought better of it. We had left behind a warm, dry house to lie in the pouring rain on a lumpy hillside.

We fell asleep for a little while but when we woke we were wet. Very, very wet. And it was absolutely nowhere near morning yet. Water was streaming over us and under us like a small river. No bivvy bag will keep you dry for long if you lie in a river. For my sins I'm quite used to miserable nights like this so I turned over to sleep some more. At which point Sarah said, 'this is a terrible idea. We are going home.' It would have been churlish, unkind and pig-headed for me to disagree. So we retreated.

The time was one minute past midnight.

'Does that mean,' Sarah asked optimistically, 'that it still counts as a microadventure?'

'Undoubtedly it was a silly experience, up there on the hill on the shortest, wettest night of the year, but as we walked back towards the dry house I still felt a buzz of happiness.'

Undoubtedly it was a silly experience, up there on the hill on the shortest, wettest night of the year, but as we walked back towards the dry house I still felt a buzz of happiness. I've walked and run over that hill many times before but I had never been up it in the dark. And at night things change: the world looks very different, it feels wilder. The few houses that still had lights on in the small village below looked like ships at sea. The sea itself was a dark void. When you're out on a boat on a night like this, the sea and sky merge into one another. Only when you see the lights of other boats do you have any sense of horizon and where the water ends and the sky begins. So it was tonight. The rain poured down. The wind blew hard. A spring tide raced up the beach, hauled up by the pull of the full moon which we could not see behind the clouds. We were walking through the darkness of a raw and wild world.

The lights on the houses accentuated how strange and wild and beautiful it feels to be outdoors in the night and how very different life feels merely by stepping outside. I ran my hand through my rain-plastered hair. We were almost back in the village. And, despite the late hour, the lack of sleep, my soaking wet jeans, and the general stupidity of it all, I felt very happy to be out there on the shortest night of the year.

I chose to keep that thought to myself.

'The lights on the houses accentuated how strange and wild and beautiful it feels to be outdoors in the night and how very different life feels merely by stepping outside.'

OTHER IDEAS LIKE THIS

Cool moons and seasonal moments worth looking out for and planning a microadventure around. Search online for precise dates:

- ⊃ Spring Equinox
- ⊃ Summer Solstice
- ⊃ Autumn Equinox
- ⊃ Winter Solstice
- ⊃ Harvest moon
- ⊃ Supermoon
- ⊃ Blue moon
- ⊃ Lunar eclipse

FROM SUMMIT TO SEA

'It's all downhill from here!' I exclaimed. We gazed around the hilltop we were about to begin our journey from.

Time Required:	Overnight
Difficulty Level:	Medium
Location:	Your county
Means of Transport:	Foot or bicycle

Starting an adventure from a high point has obvious appeal. (Forget whatever struggle it may have been to climb to the elevated spot in the first place.)

The plan was to travel from the highest point of the county to the lowest point. It is another example of making an arbitrary journey. You do not always need to have a sensible purpose for heading out on an adventure. Inventing one just to get you started is enough to ensure that you will have a unique experience.

Depending on where you live, this challenge will be very different. If you live in Norfolk, for example, you have only to climb 103 metres to the summit of Beacon Hill and then dash down less than a mile to reach the sea! (Although bear in mind that if you live in far-off Thetford, you'll have a 100-mile round trip just to get to Beacon Hill.) If you live in landlocked Leicestershire then you won't get to finish your journey at the sea, but you will begin on the summit of an extinct volcano where England's last bear is believed to have been seen.

We decided to make the trip in Cumbria, to travel from the very highest point in England all the way down to a lovely expanse of beach. We met in the pub that hosts *The World's Biggest Liar* competition (begun in honour of a pub landlord whose tall tales included the claim that local turnips grew so large that they were hollowed out to serve as cowsheds). We finished our pints, I told Tom I once climbed Scafell Pike in 33 minutes, and off we went. He was much relieved that I was not telling the truth. It actually took us a leisurely hour and a half to top out on the summit of Cumbria.

Sweaty but happy, we drew breath and took

in the view. Nothing. Nothing but cloud. But it didn't matter much. We were both flushed with the enjoyment of climbing a big hill. The last of the day's walkers had headed back down, leaving the mountain in our safe-keeping for the night. We were the highest people in England. There were 55 million Englishmen and women down there but we two were the only ones who had chosen to forsake our beds this evening to sleep on England's summit. Sheltering from the wind behind a cairn, we cooked dinner in the dusk using Tom's ingenious beer-can camping stove, a masterpiece of frugal, manly minimalism. (See page 218 if you want to make your own.)

For just a few moments the clouds parted. We glimpsed ridges around us, and a small lake far below. And then it was gone. It was almost more exciting that way, teasing us and leaving us wanting more. I fell asleep listening to Tom's in-depth explanation of the Nagorno-Karabakh dispute and the relationship between Azerbaijan and Armenia...

As if to punish me for falling asleep before he had even reached the specifics of the 1994 cease-fire,

Tom woke me at dawn by calling out, 'blue sky!'

Eagerly, I thrust my head out of my sleeping bag, just in time to see a handkerchief scrap of blue sky disappearing into the monochrome gloom of total cloud. That was the end of the blue sky. We were not going to be rewarded with a special mountain sunrise, but it was still exciting to wake on the summit of England. We began our journey to the sea. It promised to be fun: we had almost 1,000 metres of descent ahead of us!

'Sweaty but happy, we drew breath and took in the view. Nothing. Nothing but cloud. But it didn't matter much. We were both flushed with the enjoyment of climbing a big hill.'

We strolled down the hill, our packs a little heavier after filling a large bag with litter from the summit. Who are the morons who climb a mountain to savour its beauty and then think that hiding their crisp packet under a stone is acceptable? If it is you: stop it! Even banana skins and orange peel take two years to decompose, so take them away with you too. (In fact, let's begin a very simple campaign. From now on, don't just leave *no* litter in the countryside, take on the challenge of actively taking home a little bit of *extra* litter and help improve the countryside for everyone.)

We dropped beneath the clouds and all of England lay before us. We looked down Wastwater, England's deepest lake, and out just a few miles beyond it towards the coast which we could already see. This was not going to be a particularly long journey, but it was an impressive one. At the foot of the mountain we collected our bikes and set our sights on making it to the beach in time for breakfast.

The narrow, bracken-fringed road out of Wasdale must be one of the loveliest in England.

It sinews its way along the shore of Wastwater, a lake so inviting that only a stone-hearted soul could resist a swim at the foot of England's highest peak. It is, however, an eerie swim. Moments after you plunge into the cold water, the pebbled bottom drops away and all that is beneath you is blackness. It is a crystal-clear blackness, if such an oxymoron makes any sense, for the water is fresh and clear but the bottom is so far below that the water shines black like obsidian.

I have spent quite a lot of time in the Lake District but I had never followed the narrow, pretty road that winds westward from there to the sea. The point of this little trip was that it forced us to go somewhere new. For Tom, who lives in those beautiful surroundings but, by his own admission, struggles to escape the self-employed person's addiction to work, this was a fine excuse to get out of the house for some fresh air and fallow brain time. Without having this goal as an incentive, neither of us would have ventured away from our computers that day.

We freewheeled down the final mile to the Irish Sea and the small village of Seascale. The morning was quiet as we pushed our bikes down the wooden jetty. The tide was out, hundreds of metres away down the flat beach. A man walked his dog along the waterline. He was the only person on the beach. I was struck by how different this horizontal view was to the tight valleys and vertical lines of the steep mountains that ate up the sky just a couple of hours behind us.

In order to finish the trip properly, and because wild swimming is always a good addition to any microadventure, we left our bikes on the jetty and walked down the beach for a nice swim in the sea near the nuclear power station. We had made it from the summit of England to the sea before breakfast. It was a satisfying start to a day.

OTHER CHALLENGES TO TRY

The idea of taking a generic challenge and applying it to your own county, province, state or country opens up lots of possibilities.

- The highest three peaks of your county.
- The *second*-highest three peaks in Britain (it has much more solitude than the standard crowded version of Ben Nevis, Snowdon and Scafell Pike). You can then do the third-highest three peaks, the fourth and so on. I don't know which rank will be the toughest or the most beautiful, but it definitely won't be following the hordes round the most popular route.
- Create a mountain bike challenge for your county, linking popular off-road biking spots by bridleways or small roads. A good circular route could become established as a challenge in your county.
- Visit the extreme cardinal points of your county or even of Great Britain.
  North – Dunnet Head
  South – Lizard Point
  East – Lowestoft Ness
  West – Corrachadh Mòr
- Do the challenge in this chapter in reverse: from sea to summit.
- Walk from Scilly Isle to Scilly Isle at the annual low tide at the autumn equinox.

THE BIVVY CHALLENGE

33

Time Required:	Overnight
Difficulty Level:	Medium
Location:	Local
Means of Transport:	Whatever you like
Find Out More:	Watch the Video

Right. Enough reading – it's time for action.

Even the Queen, ensconced in her palace in the very heart of Britain's biggest city, is only a 15-mile yomp away from a great bivvy site in, say, the woods by the Great Pond on Epsom Common.

Nobody in the UK lives more than a few hours from somewhere green, pretty and invigorating where they can spend a night. So why not pick a warm sunny weekend and give this challenge a go?

Here are the Rules of the Bivvy Challenge:
- ➲ Your journey must start and finish at your front door.
- ➲ You must cover, through non-motorised means, a circular journey of at least 30 miles (or a distance that is moderately difficult for you).
- ➲ It must involve a night away from home.
- ➲ You must sleep outdoors (no tent) in a place you have never been before.
- ➲ You must have an outdoor swim.
- ➲ Rules are for the obedience of fools and the guidance of the wise.

Necessary Equipment:
Sleeping bag.
Bivvy bag (see pages 204–6 for equipment advice).

Not Necessary Equipment: Everything else. That's the only framework or guidance I am going to offer. The rest is up to you! Get out there, give it a go, and then share your experiences online using the #microadventure hashtag.

34 A CIRCULAR JOURNEY

This is an adventure to stir the soul. Set sail from your home, head out across the wine-dark sea and sail until you reach land.

Time Required:	2 days
Difficulty Level:	Medium
Location:	Isle of Wight
Find Out More:	Watch the Video

Then, when you disembark, brave stranger, make the choice whether you will keep the sea on your left or on your right. No other decision is necessary. Now go. Into the unknown. Go with the sea on your left, or on your right. Keep going, following that coastline, into whatever experiences and landscapes it throws up. Let the journey unfurl like the road before you. At some point will come the surprising moment when you have cycled a complete lap of the land. Your journey is complete. You can now take the boat back home to glory.

This journey could be extraordinary. Imagine making a lap of Australia, or Africa. What a journey that would be! What stories! What memories! Assuming, however, that you have neither the chutzpah nor the cash nor, possibly, even the inclination to do this, why not travel a lap of something closer to home. It could be a lake or a loch. It may be your county, or a small island. It could even be a ring road (see pages 176–81). Don't plan too much – just go.

This mini journey retains the same spirit of discovery as the epic version. All that changes is the scale and the time frame. Following any island or lake will lead you, without the need for tricky navigating, back to where you began. It makes logistics and planning very simple.

The Isle of Wight is a fine example. Late one afternoon I squeezed onto a rush hour train out of London with my folding bicycle. I felt butterflies in my stomach at the sensation of stepping into the unknown. Little matter how small the trip was, because I had no idea what lay ahead, it felt exciting.

I have never been to the Isle of Wight (except on a stag night, which I don't remember and so doesn't really count). I deliberately did no research about the island and resisted looking at tourist guides, maps or photos before I went. This may mean that I missed a 'highlight' or two, but I was willing to risk that in exchange for the surprise of the unknown.

I freewheeled down the ramp of the ferry and onto the island. This was still England, but arriving by boat made it feel more thrilling than that. Perhaps this is one of the points of microadventures – to take tiny steps which somehow feel much larger.

I pedalled up a long hill to the edge of town then stopped in a pub to eat.

'Food?!' The incredulous barmaid bounced back my innocent query. 'At this time of night?!'

It was a little after eight o'clock. I certainly was a long way from London now.

'No chance! Not for miles and miles in this direction...'

So I left the disbelieving chuckles and shakes of the head and cycled back down the long hill to the Jade Garden Chinese takeaway next to the ferry. I sat on the sea wall, eating spare ribs and watching the sun set slowly behind the town. The sky was clear and the sun a rich red. The sea reflected its colour, glowing against the silhouettes of buildings and yachts. It felt more like Havana than Hampshire.

I am always striving to teach myself to live in the 'now'. I am hopeless at it. So I cajoled myself to not worry about what would happen after sunset or where I would sleep. I wanted to just enjoy the now. I removed my watch. I challenged myself to not care about the time, about where I was or where I was going, but only to enjoy this: where I was, right

now. I wanted to relax, to be spontaneous, to slow down, to take detours. This holds true for my life in general, as well as for this microadventure.

I pottered a short way out of town and found a secluded place to sleep in long grass beneath an old chestnut tree. My bed was on top of the sea wall and the high tide lapped gently beneath me. The dusk faded as I fell asleep watching the lights of the mainland five miles away and the ships slipping down the Solent into the night.

I woke early but turned over and went back to sleep. I was taking this relaxed attitude very seriously! When I woke again the sun was a hand's breadth above the horizon, and my stomach told me that it was breakfast time. As I ambled around packing up, barefoot in the grass, an old man approached walking his very fat Labrador. We began chatting. He asked lots of questions about sleeping in a bivvy bag and about folding bicycles. I explained that I had no idea where I was going, that my only plan was to ride a lap of his island, taking as long as it took. He was amused.

'What a super idea!' he declared. 'I'm actually quite jealous.'

I invited him to join me. He laughed off the suggestion, then described where I could find the best breakfast in town.

Fuelled by fried eggs and bacon, I began my ride. I took the old chain ferry across the River Medina, wound my way past the touristy shops and curry houses of Cowes and found the sea once again. I was learning that following the sea is not as simple as it sounds. The Solent was busy with boats. Spinnakers of every colour drifted gently like balloons across the bay.

I had no map and I made a deliberate effort to never ask people how far the next town was or whereabouts I was on the island. I never knew what to expect – and that really added to the experience. I persuaded myself to not seek out shortcuts and to always stop when the inclination arose. I took photos. I walked my bike up steep hills. I rested under shady trees.

'Go with the sea on your left, or on your right. Keep going, following that coastline, into whatever experiences and landscapes it throws up. Let the journey unfurl like the road before you.'

Only now, as I write this chapter, have I looked at a map of the island. It's fun to get my bearings after the event, to discover where I rode. I remember that the area west of Cowes reminded me, bizarrely, of Hawaii or of Reykjavik. The streets were narrow and steep, with quirky clapboard homes jumbled this way and that to make the most of the access to the water or a sea view. They were painted in blues and yellows with seashells dotted around the verandas. None of this felt like the England I had left behind yesterday, the humid, antisocial pressure cooker of the London Underground.

The road took me inland, away from the sea. I was heading into the unknown, exploring, like the Antarctic explorer Vivian Fuchs or mud-streaked adventurer Bear Grylls who were both born here. 'Come, my friends, 'Tis not too late to seek a newer world' wrote Tennyson, who chose to live on the island for so long. I rode through peaceful farmland, pushing my bike up the bigger hills then zooming down the breezy descents. At times the road passed through woods, down tunnels of trees that arched and curved over the road. The dappled sunshine pooled on the tarmac and I splashed through the puddles of light.

I reached the sea again at Yarmouth. I zoomed through the town in search of a peaceful stretch of water to swim in. I was hot and sweaty and the turquoise water felt deliciously refreshing. I crunched back up the smooth shingle beach, dripping and refreshed, to dry out in the sunshine for a little while.

And then, like a true explorer, I stumbled across something completely unexpected. Something beautiful and impressive. Something that a real explorer, with a far better grasp of geography than me, would not have been in the least surprised by. I had always assumed that the Needles were down in Cornwall, so I was most surprised to find myself looking down from high cliffs at these iconic stacks of white chalk rearing out of the calm blue sea! I found myself daydreaming about what it might be like to sleep on top of the lighthouse that stood at the end of them...

'I challenged myself to not care about the time, about where I was or where I was going, but only to enjoy this: where I was, right now. I wanted to relax, to be spontaneous, to slow down, to take detours.'

I guessed, from the sun and my rumbling belly, that it was mid-afternoon, so I turned away from the Needles in search of ice cream. The road ran along high downs, beautiful with wild grasses and flowers. Gulls soared above, swooping in agitation as ramblers walking the clifftop footpath approached too close to their brood of chicks. I did not know how far I had ridden but I could no longer see the English mainland across the sea so I knew that I was round on the southern side of the island. The strong headwind was another sign that I had turned the corner.

I found my ice cream by a beach where dinosaur footprints had once been found. Refreshed, I pottered onwards. And so the day passed. I pedalled through small villages and wheat fields, through seaside towns and secluded coves. Swifts hurtled round the sky, hunting bugs, and gulls screeched and whirled behind a ploughing red

tractor. I ate fish and chips and drank a beer. A man sat beside a pier and played his accordion, busking absent-mindedly and enjoying the warmth of the setting sun on his face.

It had been a long day. I climbed up onto the downs once again. It was a beautiful evening. The grass on the cliffs was springy and soft and long enough to hide me completely when I stretched out. All that I could see was grass and the darkening sky. One or two stars appeared. I strained to stay awake for a while, enjoying looking for more stars and satellites.

'It had been a long day. I climbed up onto the downs once again. It was a beautiful evening. The grass on the cliffs was springy and soft and long enough to hide me completely when I stretched out.'

I continued my journey early the next day. Deliberately not knowing where I was and carrying no supplies meant that I had to ride through my hunger to find the next shop. My breakfast would taste all the better for that. The uncertainty also added to the excitement of seeing the first road sign for East Cowes and the end of my little circumnavigation. The end of all my exploring was to arrive where I started and to take the ferry back across the water to the mainland.

35

A RAFTING ADVENTURE

Time Required:	Overnight
Difficulty Level:	Hard
Location:	Borrowdale, Cumbria
Means of Transport:	Raft
Essential Extra Kit:	Dry bags, paddle, headtorch

It was Monday morning. I was at my desk, answering emails and listening to the radio. The DJ asked listeners to send in pictures of what they had done at the weekend. I usually ignore stuff like this. But I had enjoyed my weekend so much that I quickly submitted a couple of pictures. A few minutes later my ego received a great boost when the DJ announced to BBC 6Music's listeners that I was 'the very picture of rugged man...'

I returned to my emailing with a bit of a swagger.

One of the easiest, yet most enjoyable and interesting ways of hatching a plan for a microadventure is to simply recreate somebody else's journey. This can be done in many different ways, but two themes that lend themselves easily to replication are historical journeys (see pages 84–7) or journeys made in books (see page 247).

A while ago a friend lent me his copy of *Millican Dalton: A Search for Romance and Freedom.* (A quick aside from an author: please don't *lend* favourite books to your friends – *buy* them new copies of the books instead...) I had never heard of Millican Dalton. In 1903, aged 36, he jacked in his job as an insurance clerk in London, headed for the wild and began referring to himself as the 'Professor of Adventure'. His fabulously eccentric life after that revolved around microadventures long before hashtags were born.

Inspired by this book, I decided to head to the Lake District with my friend Tom in search of some 'hair's-breadth escapes' of my own. We would build a raft and paddle it down the River Derwent, just as the 'Professor' used to do.

Borrowdale funnels down from some of England's highest peaks to a valley of meadows alongside the river. The valley is narrow, and hills rise up on both sides of the river, craggy and covered with oak trees. As we entered the valley we were enchanted. It reminded me more of France than England. Tom trumped my comparison by likening it to Taiwan. I have never been to Taiwan, so he won the travel one-upmanship award.

We had come armed with six plastic barrels and a roll of string. Millican Dalton would probably have frowned at us. But, as well as being incompetent and needing all the help that we could get, we wanted to minimise the environmental impact of building a raft. We also had a less ambitious raft in mind than he once did: 'I discovered some felled trees lying in a wood on the shore; some of them were 35 feet long, and took five men to shift into the water.'

'The valley is narrow, and hills rise up on both sides of the river, craggy and covered with oak trees. As we entered the valley we were enchanted.'

The water level was low in the Derwent. The water was warm and trickled gently from pool to pool across riffles of pebbles. 'Hair's-breadth escapes' were extremely unlikely but a fun day in one of the loveliest valleys in the Lake Districts would do nicely in their place.

We dumped our gear on a warm pebble beach, shared our pork pie with a family of ducks, and then began to work. We spread out into the woods, searching for suitable pieces of fallen wood. We did not have a plan for how to build a raft so decided first to collect some wood and then try to figure the rest out after that.

I hauled my wood back through high bracken, privately hoping that I had found bigger stuff than Tom. I knew that this was a stupid game to be

playing; Tom is the least competitive of people and would actually be glad if I did more work than him! Returning hot and scratched, I dived into one of the river's clear pools for a quick cool off.

We constructed a frame from the longest lengths of wood, about 8 foot by 4 foot. Concerned about his knot-tying skills, I reassured Tom with the old maxim, 'if you can't tie knots, tie lots.'

From thinner, supple lengths of wood we lashed the barrels together and to the frame. We wove a

to pitch us both into the river. Then she gradually settled, sinking to a level an inch or two below the water's surface.

After some enjoyable, though farcical, attempts to paddle downstream, we had to concede defeat. It seemed as though we had diligently built a raft that didn't work. This didn't particularly matter as the building process had been so much fun. We were in our 30s but going on 13. In the process of completing the microadventures for this book I have been struck again and again by how childlike many of them feel. I mean childlike in a good way, and certainly not 'childish'. The afternoon we spent building the raft in the sunshine reminded me of my own childhood, playing beside a river in the Yorkshire Dales.

We decided to leave our stuff behind and try to make some sort of progress with the raft. Raft travel is so slow that it would not take us long to run back and collect all our gear at the end of the day. We also had to settle for taking it in turns as the raft could support one person quite happily, but not both of us. Our new plan was to punt the raft down the stream, merrily or otherwise.

We quickly gained new levels of respect for those Venetian Cornetto salesmen: punting is not as simple as it looks. Progress was very slow, but the river was beautiful and summer evenings are long. The water level was so low that there was virtually no flow to help us along. Frequently the stream was so shallow that we had to carry the raft to the next stretch of deeper water. It was very silly. And it was the most fun I had had in ages.

We had intended to drift downstream into Derwentwater and even harboured ambitions of paddling all the way across the lake. But we made such pitiful progress that, after a few hours, we settled instead for reaching the little hamlet that lay downstream. Conversation turned to the pub there and how much better beer would taste when arriving by raft.

The sky was growing darker. Night was on its way, and so too was rain. The first drops fell quickly

lattice of thin sticks through the frame to create a base to sit on and then, for ultimate rafting luxury, we piled on a thick mattress of bracken fronds to sit on. Our finished vessel looked a bit ramshackle but Poppa Neutrino, the godfather of junk rafts, would have approved. (He crossed the Atlantic on a junk raft, in case you're looking to increase the scale of your rafting exploits.) We were proud of it and excited to test it out.

She floated beautifully! We bundled all of our gear – sleeping bags, cameras, phones and wallets – into bin bags and prepared to set sail. Then, in a rare moment of common sense, we decided to actually test the raft *before* entrusting all our valuable possessions to it. It was lucky that we did for we quickly discovered that our raft did not provide sufficient buoyancy for two large adults. Accompanied by much shouting and laughing, our little Kon-Tiki wobbled furiously, threatening and suddenly. The sound of the rain grew louder. In moments the tranquil river meander became more like a wild jungle as the full force of the storm crashed over us. The pelting rain was warm and Tom and I laughed and whooped as the rain rattled furiously over the surface of the river and soaked us to the skin. It was a savage and magical experience. The storm passed just as we arrived at the village. We left the raft on the riverbank and headed for a pub. We were bedraggled and grinning as we walked up the deserted road in search of beer and shelter.

But there was no pub! What sort of English village doesn't have a pub?! Fortunately we were both in such good spirits that we were not too disheartened.

The rain had passed now and the evening was cool and fresh as we headed back upstream to collect our kit and then search for Millican Dalton's cave. Tucked away in the woods, halfway up a craggy hillside, the Professor of Adventure lived in a large cavern for decades. We wanted to find it and spend a night there. We arrived at the cave as dusk was falling, emerging from the dripping woods into a clearing with views across to the steaming hillside on the other side of the river.

We turned on our torches then plunged through tall wet bracken into the dark opening of the cave. We hoped that it was dry inside because the night outside promised to be very wet. Millican's cave was much larger than I had expected, stretching perhaps 15 metres in each direction and, mercifully, it was dry. I have spent many nights camping in strange places of the world and yet, I confided to Tom, I would have felt nervous sleeping in that cave by myself. The mind can play funny tricks on you. It was good to have company.

I was so hungry that I was even looking forward to our dinner of out-of-date couscous ('Only 2.5p per pack!' Tom had boasted that morning) and a can of petrol station stew. I watched the blue flames licking the pan and listened to the incessant dripping of water at the cave's entrance. When we needed more water we placed our metal mug

beneath one of the drips. The ding-ding-ding of metallic splashes decreased as the cup gradually filled with water.

We unfurled our sleeping bags on the flat cave floor. It was a peaceful haven and a perfect hideaway from the rain which fell in floods through the warm summer night.

Building a raft and sleeping in a cave added up to a really memorable day. Without having read *Millican Dalton: A Search for Romance and Freedom* I would not have gone to Borrowdale. That is one good reason for retracing a historical or literary journey, but another is that it adds an extra layer to the experience. Tom and I would have enjoyed our rafting journey regardless of Millican Dalton's influence. However, we enjoyed it even more knowing that, 100 years ago, another mildly eccentric man in his 30s had chosen to escape the rat race and seek solitude and wilderness out here on the exact same stretch of river. The views that the three of us enjoyed are identical even a century apart, as was our enjoyment of paddling very slowly through the countryside.

36

A MOUNTAIN ADVENTURE

As your confidence in microadventures grows, you'll be pleased to discover that there are challenges and adventures that are at the very limit of your capabilities right here in Britain - you just need to find them.

Time Required:	2 days
Difficulty Level:	Hard
Location:	Skye
Means of Transport:	Foot, bicycle and boat
Essential Extra Kit:	Climbing gear
Find Out More:	Watch the Video

A mere 12km of walking on the hilltops of Britain doesn't sound much, but it looked impressive: my first sight of the Cuillin Ridge was from many miles away, across the sea on the Bealach na Bà, looking over the water towards those far blue mountains. I was heading to the Isle of Skye on a whim to climb dangerous mountains with a man I'd never met. He had read some of my books then emailed me after we both entered a stupid winter mountain bike race (see pages 48–50). He won the race. I just about survived it.

But Alex's idea had appealed immediately: to mountain bike cross-country to the sea, paddle

over the sea to the mountains, and then attempt the formidable Cuillin Ridge. A triathlon of challenging microadventures through some of the finest landscapes in Britain? I'm on my way, I replied.

So we began from the pub at Sligachan, pedalling happily up the glen, excited to be on the move, and delighted by the weather which appeared to be holding and which was crucial to our success. The path was narrow single-track, strewn with rocks and ditches. I quickly realised that the mountain biking hills of Surrey are inadequate preparation for the skill levels needed for the Scottish Highlands. However, in between my stumbles, foot-downs, and a comic straight-over-the-handlebars-into-a-bog, I relished the beautiful, remote riding.

On all sides barren peaks rose from the glen into a warm sky. And silence. I remember the

silence. The silence was so intense that it was almost oppressive. We passed a loch, perfect for a swim, but we had miles to go before nightfall so we pressed on instead, hurtling down an exhilarating descent to a sweeping bay. The isolation was accentuated by a single white house, built bang in the middle of the curving bay, far from electricity or running water. It would be a wonderful house in which to spend time with friends, running up hills, drinking beer, hatching grand plans and cooking mussels gathered from the beach.

But today we rode onwards, up a bugger of a hill and blasted, whooping, down the other side, down to a tight little bay and the beginning of the second phase of our triathlon microadventure. We were going to paddle out into the sea, across the bay, to the base of the impressive mountain range before

'The path was narrow single-track, strewn with rocks and ditches. I quickly realised that the mountain biking hills of Surrey are inadequate preparation for the skill levels needed for the Scottish Highlands.'

us. Whilst I inflated my beloved packraft, Alex chatted with his friend Colin who'd met us here, armed with a couple of sea kayaks.

I acknowledge that it is not in the spirit of microadventures to need to rely on a man with a van and a couple of spare sea kayaks! But the day was hot and the paddle was a joy, a perfect burst of

sea fever. It was a windy day with the white clouds flying and the flung spray, the blown spume and the seagulls crying. Waves cooled my face and soaked my clothes as the blunt packraft battered the swell.

It is a special thing, being in a boat. Your view is a privileged one, inaccessible to those mere mortals left behind on the shore. The mountains ahead of us looked serene and stupidly exciting. Jellyfish pulsed as they drifted, pretty pink and white, through the clear blue brine. The shore gradually receded behind us. Blisters bubbled on my hands but the mountains loomed a little larger with each small stroke of the paddle. The headwind made progress difficult. We were paddling westward into the dazzling evening sun. Liquid stars fell from our paddles and burst over the bows of my boat.

'Today we rode onwards, up a bugger of a hill and blasted, whooping, down the other side, down to a tight little bay and the beginning of the second phase of our triathlon microadventure.'

At last, tired, wet, but happy, we reached the lee of the mountains. Sheltered from the headwind we could lie back in our boats and relax for a few moments. We were in the mouth of a secluded sea loch, tucked tight into a brooding cleft at the base of the mountains that thrust steeply straight up from the shore. The Cuillins are the ancient eroded remains of a vast volcano lip and they curved spectacularly above us, jagged and menacing like rotted black stumps of teeth.

It is hard to imagine a more beautiful paddle in Britain, and I grinned in delight once again at my decision to begin searching for wildness and adventure here in my own country. Alex was thrilled as well. Although he knew Skye well and was a regular climber and mountain biker here, he had never experienced a paddle such as this. Britain is a beautiful and wild country. Even in your backyard there are new adventures, new sights, new perspectives: you just have to make the small effort to go and discover them.

Alex pointed behind me and I turned to look. A dozen seals were peering curiously at us with damp dark eyes. Two snorted and dived. The rest watched quizzically as we paddled gently to the shore past a couple of seal pups still in their juvenile white fur. Two terns, the whitest and sleekest of sea birds, shrieked and dived at us, concerned for the young in their nests. We, though, were concerned only for food. We had been on the move for a long time and were very hungry. We pulled our boats up onto the shore beside a small river.

While Alex cooked up a big pan of pasta, I went for a quick walk. I followed the course of the Scavaig River, one of Britain's shortest rivers. I followed it up from the sea for just a couple of hundred metres to its beginning in Loch Coruisk. I had wanted to visit this loch for years and I was grinning with excitement to be here. It is an extraordinarily remote, atmospheric and beautiful spot.

We slept on the shore until, much too soon, the alarm on my watch woke us up. It was 3am. Time to begin the third phase of our adventure: tackling

'At last, tired, wet, but happy, we reached the lee of the mountains. Sheltered from the headwind we could lie back in our boats and relax for a few moments.'

the famous Cuillin Ridge that would lead us back to the pub where we had started. We hoped to reach it in time for last orders. Only 12km of ridge stood between us and beer, and yet we had allowed 20 hours to get there. That should give an indication of the difficulties that stood in our way.

We left Colin sleeping (he would paddle home later towing the spare kayak) and Alex and I began climbing through the darkness. By sunrise we were atop the first Munro of the day, enjoying

across a gap, then turned back to look at me. His face was a little pale.

'I recommend you don't look here – just jump.'

I jumped.

Then I turned round to see what I had jumped over. I looked down.

It was a long, long way down.

Deep breath.

Push on. Keep going.

My admiration for the people who run the length of the ridge in just three and a half hours turned to amazement as we reached the first climbing section. These mountain madmen scamper, un-roped, up and down cliffs which, to my wimpish eye, looked absolutely terrifying. I was extremely happy to be roped up as we wriggled our way up very difficult (V Diff) and mild severe (MS) rock faces and abseiled down the other side. These climbing sections were the only likely things to stop us finishing our challenge, so we were chuffed to be ticking them off.

I am no climber and I do not intend to become one. I love the literature but not the life expectancy. I enjoyed the puzzle and the challenge of climbing – the riddle of hand and feet combinations to heave yourself up a vertical face – but I did so with very little enthusiasm for looking down between my feet to enjoy the view. The technical term for this yawning empty space is 'Exposure'. I do not like Exposure one bit! But I found it fascinating to face this fear. I was tied securely to a rope – I was safe – but I did not feel safe. And that alone meant that this was a perfect microadventure: I was out of my comfort zone even in a relatively safe place and I was pushing myself hard, mentally and physically. I was learning about myself and peeling back my boundaries.

The most spectacular spot on the ridge is the marvellously-named Inaccessible Pinnacle. It's described in the book *Wild Places* by Robert MacFarlane as 'a shark's fin of black rock that jags hundreds of feet out of the ridge which had long been, to my mind, one of the wildest points in the

a staggeringly beautiful view of mountains, sea and islands.

This summit – Gars-bheinn – serves as the start point of the ridge challenge. We began at a good speed and in high spirits. The weather was beautiful. We had made a really early start so everything was looking promising. We made good speed for a couple of hours, hiking, jumping and scrambling along the ridge. On both sides was sky, a lot of sky, and a long, long way to fall. The views were as beautiful as from an aeroplane. I have rarely been anywhere as beautiful. But we could spare only a few glances; full attention was needed to concentrate on our footing and route finding at all times. It may seem strange that route finding is difficult high on an exposed ridge, but it was such a jumbled rocky chaos up there and progress was hellish hard. At one point Alex paused, leaped

world... a knife-edge ridge with an overhanging and infinite drop on one side, and a drop on the other side even steeper and longer.'

The Inaccessible Pinnacle was the symbolic high point of the challenge. The view from the top was extraordinary, even if I was clinging to the rock with a vice-like grip. These are the moments that make you feel most alive.

But despite my jubilation and general 'aliveness' my knee unfortunately reacted badly to the contorted terrain. After eight hours on the ridge I was moving like an old man after twisting my knee. There was no way I would be able to make it the whole way. We were forced to limp down from the ridge and concede defeat.

'The view from the top was extraordinary, even if I was clinging to the rock with a vice-like grip. These are the moments that make you feel most alive.'

I was not happy to have failed, especially through something as random and uncontrollable as an injury. The triathlon microadventure challenge had been such a good one. I was disappointed to have let Alex down but I was also quite impressed to have failed. Britain is not a particularly rugged place. You don't tend to get beaten by the landscapes, so I gained a twisted satisfaction at being humbled by these ancient, awesome mountains. I had underestimated them.

Mountains do not care how you fare on their slopes and summits. They were around for millions of years before your petty quests began, and they'll still be standing – beautiful yet uncaring – when our grandchildren's grandchildren feel the same restless, timeless urge to test themselves.

Sure, go and pit your wits, your skills, your guts, your luck against them. You might win, you might lose, but they don't care either way. Maybe that's part of their appeal. It's certainly a good metaphor for doing big stuff in life: do it for the doing, not for the praise of others. Don't be put off trying big stuff by the fear of failure. The mountains don't think any less of me because I failed. They neither fête me if I triumph, nor sneer if I fail. And those mountains are a far better judge than the office jobsworth whiner who sneers and mocks people who fail.

So I failed this microadventure, but I have great memories that would not be there had I not even begun. I also now have an excuse, should one be needed, to return soon to the wild places of Skye for some unfinished business.

ALSO TRY THESE OTHER RIDGE CHALLENGES

Make sure you are suitably competent, levelheaded and equipped to be able to tackle these potentially dangerous routes. If you'd like to learn to climb, search online for the British Mountaineering Council who will be able to point you in the right direction. Those in the South East might also be interested to search online for the London Mountaineer mini guide.

- Craig y Fan Ddu, Brecon Beacons.
- Crib Goch, Snowdonia.
- The Coledale Horseshoe, Lake District.
- Aonach Eagach Ridge, Glencoe.
- Rum Cuillin traverse, Inner Hebrides.

37 A JOURNEY TO THE END OF MY COUNTRY

Early that morning I looked just like everybody else. I pedalled steadily along the Euston Road in London along with all the commuters.

Time Required:	Several days
Difficulty Level:	Hard
Location:	Shetland Isles
Means of Transport:	Bike and packraft
Find Out More:	Watch the Video

My folding Brompton bicycle was perfect for the job in hand. A gem of British engineering, its tiny wheels zipped happily along the tarmac. At the station I met my friend, Joe. We folded our bikes in seconds and squeezed aboard the crowded train. The only clue, perhaps, that our day was not going to be the same as everyone else's were the canoe paddles sticking up out of our rucksacks and our excited grins – because we were off on an adventure!

Granted, it was a very small adventure, but ever since I began taking on these intentionally small 'expeditions', I have discovered that coming up with an interesting plan (and committing to making it happen) is virtually all you need to do to guarantee an interesting, challenging and rewarding experience. For someone cursed with eternal '*fernweh*' (a beautiful German word meaning 'a craving for distant places'), microadventures have been an excellent tonic.

We unfolded our new map as the train rattled north. Names like The Slithers, Bluemull Sound and Muckle Flugga sparked my curiosity amongst the wiggling, jagged cartography of islands, inlets and hilltops of the Shetland Isles. It was fitting to spot Muckle Flugga on my map, for this was where this trip began. Actually, it began at Lord's Cricket Ground. Or, more precisely still, it began at home one day when I heard a radio interview on Test Match Special with a lighthouse keeper from the Shetland Isles who had come to watch the cricket on his first ever visit to London. In a soft, lilting dialect – almost more Norwegian than Scottish – he told how he had often listened to cricket matches as colossal waves crashed upon Britain's most northerly lighthouse on the storm-lashed rock of Muckle Flugga. Muckle Flugga! What a beautiful name! And I had never heard of it.

'For someone cursed with eternal "fernweh", microadventures have been an excellent tonic.'

I reached for my biggest atlas and there it was – 'Muckle Flugga' – farther north than St Petersburg or Helsinki, a tiny island off the north coast of Uist which is the most northerly of the main Shetland Islands. It was 100 miles north of John O'Groats, my previous benchmark for the extreme north of the UK. Muckle Flugga really marked the very top of my country. Not only had I never heard of it, I had never *been* there. I began planning...

Eventually we traded train for ferry. Joe and I wheeled our little bikes into the big belly of the overnight ferry from Aberdeen to the Shetland Isles. Our plan was simple, as good adventures ought to be. The best adventures are those that ring true, that can be summarised in a sentence or two, and planned on the back of a receipt from your book and map shop. We would travel from the south of the island chain all the way to the north. No buses, no ferries. We would pedal the length of each island then fold up our bikes and paddle by packraft across to the next island in this little northern archipelago.

I fell asleep on the ferry reading *The Odyssey*. Tell me, Muse, the story of that man who was driven to wander far and wide... The irony of reading the epic *Odyssey* on a microadventure was not lost on me. But you don't need to deal with a cyclops giant or the Siren's song to have an adventure. All you need is something challenging, somewhere new, and a bit of imagination.

Arriving in Lerwick by ferry after 14 hours at sea, it was easy to imagine that we were in some exciting, foreign country. But no, despite the long journey and the wanderlust fizzing in my belly, this was still home. The cafes still sold bacon and eggs and big sweet mugs of tea.

We were ready to ride. We began at Sumburgh Head, pedalling north on a blustery summer's day on our overladen, underpowered bikes. Strapped to the bikes were tents and sleeping bags and all the equipment we needed for paddling between the islands. I have little tolerance for gimmick expeditions and I worried if perhaps I had crossed the line here. Why packraft when there's a ferry? (Particularly a ferry which can transport livestock at the price of 70p per head!) But virtually all expeditions have a measure of artificiality to them, deliberately making things more difficult than they need to be in return for the thrill of success against the odds. So I think I squeezed in beneath the Novelty Contrived Adventure radar. Just.

This mighty three-day microadventure was my longest bike journey since I finished cycling round the world. We passed a signpost marking the latitude of 60 degrees North. The Shetlands are closer to the Arctic than parts of Alaska. We were closer to five other capital cities than to London. The sensation of isolation and distance was palpable.

Fat seals basked on beaches. At our approach they flopped down the sand to the sanctuary of the pale blue bay where they raised their eyes above the water and watched us carefully until we remounted our 3-speed bikes and wobbled away.

Throughout our ride the sea would appear at surprising times and in surprising places: we were never more than three miles from the sea anywhere

'Our plan was simple, as good adventures ought to be. The best adventures are those that ring true, that can be summarised in a sentence or two, and planned on the back of a receipt from your book and map shop.'

on the Shetlands. Long-fingered fjords (known locally as 'voes') probed all around, appearing first to our left, then to our right. By evening the skies were heavy and the voes dull gunmetal grey. The half-light felt calming, charming, and soothing, as did the tiny hamlets we passed through.

In one sheltered voe a group of women were preparing for an evening outing in a solid old-fashioned rowing boat. They were fitting oars to rowlocks, chattering, and clambering aboard. They called to us, asking if we wanted to join them. I said 'no thanks': always the worst reply to give to invitations when travelling, and immediately regretted it as their boat pulled gently out into the still bay.

It looked an idyllic way to relax after what probably had not actually been a very stressful day for them. I thought of rush hour on the London Underground and wondered why I was not living up here instead. This question turned over and over in my mind throughout the trip. I tried to work out whether I would be very happy or very bored living in one of these tiny communities. Probably both.

A lovely thing about summer journeys in the North is that you can potter and faff to your heart's content and still not run out of daylight. We pitched our tent and cooked dinner in broad daylight beside a bronze peat stream at 11pm. Long hours of daylight also means there is no hurry to leap out of your sleeping bag at early o'clock. It's a civilised sort of adventuring, though it feels less so when you wake to the familiar Scottish drumroll of rain on the tent. We rode on in the rain, considerably less in love with the Shetland Isles than we had been yesterday.

The weather was not just an excuse to be miserable, it was also a cause for concern. Today we needed to take to the sea, paddling across the strong tides of Yell Sound to the next island. As we stood by the waves I felt very anxious. The current was flowing fast, the wind was brisk, and we could not see the far shore. The slate grey sea was foreboding. This was to be my first foray onto the sea in my packraft. We folded the bikes, lashed

them to our rafts and, on the slack of the tide, paddled tentatively out into the Sound. I was full of doubt as to how far we would get. (Note: this was a pretty stupid activity and one I absolutely don't recommend!)

'We pitched our tent and cooked dinner in broad daylight beside a bronze peat stream at 11pm.'

We made good progress until the tide began to race once more, at which point we could make no further leeway. We bolted for the sanctuary of a small, uninhabited island. There we pitched the tent beside a dilapidated croft and shivered in wet clothes for a few hours. We were waiting for the tide to slow and – hopefully – the fog to clear sufficiently for us to see the island of Yell that we were heading for. It was unnerving to paddle without being able to see where we were heading. I read *The Odyssey* and dozed until it was time to try again.

Scudding rainy drifts vexed the dim sea as we began. But at least we had caught an important glimpse of land through the mist which confirmed what we knew from our map: Yell lay that way, and it really was not very far away, across the gloom of the dark, broad sea. It helped ease our fears. The paddle was quite easy in the end, even though it was through heavy evening rain. We were wet but happy, excited at having taken on something that frightened us and then carried it out successfully. So we paddled nonchalantly up the shoreline of Yell for an extra mile or two, just for the fun of it, relishing the calm evening and the occasional rising seal.

When you are soaked to the bone there is only one option for the self-respecting microadventurer (as opposed to the ascetic, masochistic zealot of my youth): we headed to the Hilltop Bar, 'Britain's Most Northerly Pub', and draped our sodden gear across their radiators. (Though we are not now that strength which in old days moved heaven and earth, that which we are, we are...)

The landlady clucked pityingly over us and called us fools to even be contemplating tomorrow's paddle across the notorious Bluemull Sound. Soon we heard the pleasing 'ding' of the kitchen microwave – common to many rural Scottish dining experiences – and all felt better with the world as we tucked into plates of nuclear-hot scampi.

As well as their charming accent and their obsession with the weather (even by British standards), I was struck by the locals' proud love for their remote lives. A mechanic from the crab-canning factory was also the island's mobile DJ, putting on discos in village halls in his spare time. He would have scoffed had I mentioned David Cameron's much-mocked 'Big Society' ideas, but that is how life really works in small communities. A major highlight here was 'Chinese Night'

when, once or twice a month, Lerwick's Chinese Restaurant takes to the road in a caravan and cooks up a taste of the East on the different islands. Chewing long and hard on my scampi, I could understand the appeal.

'Sunshine!' shouted Joe, unzipping the tent. Instantly I was awake and happy. Few places on Earth can beat the beauty of Scotland on the rare occasions when the sun is shining and there are no midges. In summer-holiday mood we pedalled the meandering narrow roads of Yell towards our next paddle and the one that worried me most. Bluemull Sound is only a narrow stretch of sea but currents can race through at up to 14 knots: way beyond the capabilities of packrafts.

Fortunately the tides were calm and we paddled easily across the still water in jubilant mood.

Paddling round rocky coves we saw seals and sea otters as well as thousands of birds. We had reached Unst, Britain's most northerly inhabited island. Nothing could stop us now. Beaching the boats, we dived into the cold clear water for a celebratory swim.

Unst was my favourite island. There was a palpable atmosphere of calm living. Yellow meadow flowers waved in the gentle breeze, grazed by eponymous ponies. Hills rolled ahead of us. On all sides was water and tiny islands studded the glimmering sea. Small homes scattered up the flanks of green fells. Even the bus shelter had character, decorated eccentrically and a noted tourist attraction.

'The lighthouse began to twinkle from the rocks. The long day wanes. I stood outside my tent in the soft solstice midnight light looking out to sea.'

We soon reached the end of the road, for all the distances were tiny on this microadventure. We pushed our bicycles cross-country, up a hill, through a bog, and onwards until we stood and whooped on the north coast's cliffs. Puffins bustled overhead or veered crazily in to land, wings flapping desperately, orange feet splayed as they reached for grip on the cliff. Gannets and skuas swirled in the wind. A small islet was completely white with guano and seabirds. The cacophony of the colony mingled with the noise of the turquoise waves smashing below us and against Muckle Flugga. We had made it! It was only a rocky outcrop in the sea, only a lighthouse: these were pretty unremarkable things to have travelled 900 miles to see. And yet, without a doubt, the journey to the end of my country had been a pleasure, an education, and an adventure.

The lighthouse began to twinkle from the rocks. The long day waned. I stood outside my tent in the soft solstice midnight light looking out to sea. I was at the very top of Britain. I realised that only now was I beginning to understand how little I know of my own country.

Our tent was pitched on a patch of grass that was as flat and green as a snooker table. A single pace away from the tent was the cliff edge. The only sounds were birds and waves. Not only was it one of the best camping spots I have enjoyed in Britain, it was one of the best in the world. You don't need much time or money or expertise to experience a night's camping like that. You just need to go and do it.

AN M25 ADVENTURE

38

To prove the point that microadventure is more about attitude and imagination than having access to great wilderness, I decided to seek adventure in the most boring place I could think of.

Time Required:	One Week
Difficulty Level:	Hard
Location:	The M25
Means of Transport:	Foot

When I phoned my friend Rob to invite him along he said, 'That's a stupid idea. Let's do it!'

And so we set out together to walk a lap of the M25 motorway.

The M25 is a 120-mile monstrosity encircling London, the original road to hell. Everyone hates the M25; it sums up much of what is tedious about modern life. Traffic-snared and frustrating for motorists, its route through the commuter lands promised little better for the intrepid hiker. Our plan was to walk as close to the motorway as possible, from Junction 1 to Junction 31. The route would take us from Kent to Essex via Surrey, Berkshire, Buckinghamshire and Hertfordshire. We would walk through fields and towns, golf courses and housing estates, down footpaths if we saw them, along occasional small parallel roads from time to time. We deliberately had no real plan. It seemed likely that we would end up walking somewhere between 150 and 200 miles. We had a week available to complete the journey and we carried just one small-scale map of the whole motorway. You don't really need more than that when you are just planning to follow your nose alongside a massive road. We ate in chip shops and

drank tea in greasy spoon cafes. At night we would sleep outside, in bivvy bags, despite the snow that lay thick on the ground. For, completely by chance, we had chosen the coldest week of the worst winter in 30 years to undertake our adventure. It turned into a Siberian suburban experience. So we hoped that we might also find occasional refuge under a bridge, in a barn, or in the home of a kind stranger.

It was dawn. Snow was falling. Rob and I were in a cheerless industrial estate on the south bank of the Thames estuary. Above us arched the impressive span of the Queen Elizabeth II Bridge, gridlocked with traffic creeping towards the tollbooths at Junction 1 of the M25. It was the first working day after the New Year holidays and

'Oi, mate, shut the bleedin' door!'

We explained what we were doing and they laughed and said that we were crazy.

'Two sugars or three?'

Crazy, maybe, but the M25 turned out to be a genuinely interesting and difficult adventure. It was physically tough. We discovered interesting new places and pockets of surprising beauty. Reigate and Rickmansworth are hardly Timbuktu or Ulan Bator, but walking round the M25 honestly ticked all the same boxes of adventure that cycling round the world did.

'Walking the M25?! Are you mad?'

'Well it should be quicker than driving.'

'In this weather? Rather you than me...'

It made people chuckle, made them roll their eyes at our folly, made folks wrap their arms round themselves and be glad they would soon be in their warm car and sleeping in their warm bed tonight. Builders, old men, a young couple: all thought we were mad, that our idea was ridiculous, and that doing it during the worst winter in a generation sealed our insanity.

But our walk was an instant opening into conversation. We were bombarded from all sides with questions, incredulity and good-humoured mocking. We made so many attempts over the next week to explain ourselves. To say that we were looking for a challenging adventure right here on our doorsteps, that we wanted to learn more about our own country, meet interesting people and test ourselves.

A bacon butty and a mug of tea arrived. Our hats and gloves steamed on the radiators. But what really warmed us and quickened our stride back towards the M25 were the wishes of goodwill, the laughter we had created, and the feeling that we really were on an adventure. As on all good journeys, we knew we must not rush and that we should have the openness to talk to everyone.

Eventually, round about lunchtime and Junction 2, we broke free of Dartford and its satellite sprawl. We left behind the housing

everything about the scene was gloomy and dull. I began to feel that this was not such a great idea after all. I tried to look on the bright side: a week from now we should be finished.

It is not very easy to walk a lap of the M25. It is, understandably, hardly geared towards pedestrians. Slip roads and flyovers and high fences continually blocked our route. We began walking down pavements and through housing estates, across wasteland and through hedges. It was surprisingly difficult to make forward progress. But on the corner of Main Street, a cafe confirmed all my hopes about this trip. People in hiking gear with large packs on their backs were evidently not the cafe's usual customers.

estates and cul-de-sacs and jumped fences through scrubby fields watched only by Travellers' ponies: we had reached the countryside.

I always like standing under a motorway bridge. Above you the huddled masses race madly in both directions, 24 hours a day, yearning to be free. Down below, unseen by the world, we sheltered from the snow beneath the massive slabs of concrete. Rob removed his boots to tend to his already-sore feet. I glanced over the repetitive, basic graffiti tags of bored youths who had been here signing proof of their repetitive, basic lives, kicking cans through puddles, smoking fags, boasting of women and Saturday nights. I'd love somehow to take them out for a night on a hill and a new perspective.

'Completely by chance, we had chosen the coldest week of the worst winter in 30 years to undertake our adventure.'

It was only early afternoon but the light was already seeping from the monochrome January day. Britain was returning to work after the New Year festivities. We were getting back into the mindset and rhythm of life in the outdoors. Modern life is played out in permanent sterility. We live in the light until we choose some hours of darkness. Temperatures remain the same all year, even as the seasons outside rotate through their cycle. The fridge preserves what used to be seasonal foods, taps give water, and the warmth and refuge of our beds await us each night of the year.

But Rob and I were having to return to the old ways, the daily forage for food and water, the challenge to keep warm and dry in response to the whims of the day's weather, and the mild anxiety of seeking safe shelter each night. All this played out just miles from central London, within the strict constraints of the hours of daylight which in

January, we were remembering, limited us to only about nine hours of action each day.

We tramped through white fields, their silence emphasised by the continual drone of the nearby motorway. Even that seemed muffled by the snowfall. Pylons loomed in the gloom. It was a disorientating, fantastical feeling crunching across the snow-covered stubble of fallow fields. We had no idea where we were or what lay ahead of us. But it mattered little so long as we were following our road.

At nightfall we lashed a poncho between two trees to create a basha. Home sweet home! We lay in our sleeping bags eating Super Noodles and feeling well with the world. It is amazing how your mood rises once you are warm and tucked up in bed, even if your bed is a bivvy bag in a snowy wood beside Junction 3 of the M25.

The motorway did not sleep. Cars and lorries roared restlessly through the night. Each time I woke, I glanced at the moon. Its progress across the sky gave me a rough idea of how long I had been asleep. I glanced towards the motorway as well. It was always alive and moving. The only disturbance through the long night was a fox. He grabbed his chance and crept up to try to steal our bag of food. Hungry times for wild animals. Hungry times for long-distance walkers too, so I shooed him away and he slunk into the night.

One of the pleasant aspects of a winter expedition is the amount of sleep you can have. Twelve hours after going to bed our alarm sounded. The stars were blazing in the cold pre-dawn darkness. The ground was covered with the tracks of rabbits, foxes and birds, clues to the nocturnal world we did not know. No longer did this feel like a human-dominated world. It was as though we had moved to a forest in Siberia or flown centuries back in time to medieval Kent.

We pushed and ducked under bushes and tree branches bowed down with snow. I jumped up to grab a branch and showered Rob with snow. His curses and my laughter were the only sound, apart from the road. We could see no sign of mankind.

Ours were the only human footprints. We were alone in the wild, about 20 metres away from thousands of people on the motorway.

Our idyll was rather spoiled by the realisation that in order to cover the requisite four junctions per day, we would have to trek into the night. So each day we just kept on walking through the frozen darkness until we had covered sufficient distance. We started each day at 6am and our latest finish was 11pm. We arrived in Redhill – Junction 8 – late at night. Rob was chuntering about how he could walk back home in just a few hours from here. We were cold and tired. So we headed to a pub for some morale-boosting food.

The barmaid poured us a free beer and a kind couple, Ronan and Helen, rescued us from a night sleeping in the snow by inviting us to stay at their house. As well as being thrilled at the prospect of a shower and a warm sleep, we were delighted to discover that the kind strangers who have helped Rob and me so often in distant lands also live in suburban England. The strongest memories of all adventures tend to be the people you meet along the way.

Kindness followed us on our journey. A man called Matt, who knew our whereabouts from Twitter, came out on his bike to find us early one morning and invite us for a fried breakfast at his home. We were discovering that if you just break away from the norm a little bit and do something different and interesting then people will respond, wherever you are in the world.

We crossed the Thames – a halfway point of sorts – and planes rumbled loudly over our heads as we ate a sandwich on the pavement close to Heathrow. The days were settling into a steady routine, as they always do on expeditions.

We had learned the importance of pubs as hubs of conversation and community on this journey. So one evening when we were really flagging we headed to one near Rickmansworth (Junction 17). A lady bought us brandy and the pub band dedicated a song to us, 'These boots are made for walking'.

A city trader finished his pint, walked over to us and said we could camp on his snow-covered lawn. He didn't quite feel comfortable enough to ask us into his family home, but he did come out at 6am, in his boxer shorts, with mugs of hot tea to wish us well for our journey.

One morning Rob found a discarded child's sledge. He loaded our packs onto it to tow as though we were on our way to the South Pole. Screwing up my face against the icy wind, I hauled the sledge through the white landscape. I was tired and cold but after so many years of reading books and dreaming of Antarctica, I finally felt like Captain Scott! Instead of Antarctica, though, we were trekking through Hertfordshire, somewhere around Junction 19.

Some time later the sledge broke and Rob moved on to a shopping trolley, wheeling his belongings through the grey streets like a character from Cormac McCarthy's novel *The Road*. A lady walking her dog lowered her gaze, crossed the road, and walked by at speed. We were degenerating towards hobo status.

Our daily staple of ketchup sandwiches was wearing a little thin so we set our sights on the luxuries of South Mimms service station. Walking through the darkness, we fantasised about warmth and food. We clambered through a frightening junkyard filled with threatening signs about guard dogs. We were lost, stumbling around in the night trying to find a way to cross the A1 and get into the service station. We eventually succeeded and wearily arrived at the bright lights of the service station with more elation than most people there would have felt.

Not content to just eat dinner in the service station, we decided to sleep in some bushes in the car park so that we could get an early breakfast there too. Eating breakfast, I noticed that people avoided my gaze; without my pack to explain my dirty dishevelled appearance I looked wild and strange and scary.

'We were getting back into the mindset and rhythm of life in the outdoors. Modern life is played out in permanent sterility. We live in the light until we choose some hours of darkness.'

In Essex the temperatures rose a little, leaving us trudging along slushy paths. We slipped plastic shopping bags over our socks to keep our feet dry. Our sleeping bags were damp, our feet sore and we lapsed into a bit of good old-fashioned whinging and moaning. A lady who was sweeping out a stable block spotted us and made us a cup of tea.

'My son's mad like you two. He loves adventure,' she said, stirring the tea. 'A hot drink will do you good.'

The variety of landscapes, natural and man-made, that we encountered walking through six counties was surprisingly interesting. I was also struck by how clear was the separation between the different types of people whose homes we walked past. The Surrey gentry, clusters of Sikhs, white working class, North London boys done good and moved to suburbia... There was often only a very short distance separating the different groups, but the dividing lines were clear cut.

The M25 walk was through an environment very much controlled by man, but I relished feeling the forces of nature at work as well. We can build highways that transport millions of people and tonnes of manufactured goods right through the night. We can blot out the stars with the glow of streetlights, but we cannot control the land being covered in snow. Snow that reflected the orange glow so that even at night it was light enough to see and walk cross-country. Nor can we control the biting wind which nipped our noses and ears and had us hankering for shelter. Down to our right, the pouring stream of red and white lights raced on. Nobody knew we were out here and I liked that feeling of anonymity.

After a week of hard walking the vast columns of the Queen Elizabeth II Bridge straddling the Thames came into view again. We had walked all 31 junctions of the M25. Our circle was virtually complete.

The snow, the wild camping, the kebab shops, the fence-jumping, the shopping trolley: it had been quite a week. We were very tired but also more jubilant than we could have imagined. We had successfully found adventure in modern, built-up England. We had scratched our curiosity and proved that if you step just a fraction away from the main road, away from the conventional route that everyone else is taking and the road you have always taken, then you can see things differently. You can challenge yourself and have novel, interesting experiences.

It's not an easy route, for sure. There are no signposts on the road less-travelled, nobody to advise you, no idea what lies round the next bend. But if you don't care where the road is going, nor what awaits you, and instead are curious to find out, then this is a great way to walk for a while.

All that remained was to cross the bridge and complete our circle. We knew that we could not walk across the bridge, but had heard rumours that the Transport Police would give a lift to pedestrians and cyclists. At the bridge we found a phone that was a direct line to request a lift across. We were so near the end. Eager for a shower, for hot food, for home.

'Sorry', the man on the other end of the phone told us. 'We're only allowed to take cyclists across these days. No walkers allowed.'

'Why?' we asked.

'Health and Safety, mate.'

It felt like the perfect end to a modern microadventure.

HOW TO HAVE YOUR OWN MICROADVENTURE

CALENDAR OF THE MICROADVENTURE YEAR

Use this calendar to help you concoct seasonal microadventure ideas of your own to do over the course of a year.

You can search online for more details about each entry. Jotting down your own ideas in the margins of the appropriate month will make it easier for you to plan, commit and actually make stuff happen...

Remember that in each month there will be a full moon and a new moon, and spring and neap tides. These are also good things to plan microadventures around.

You can also find this calendar online at www.alastairhumphreys.com/?p=13567 if you'd like to print out copies.

JANUARY

- New Year's Day swim in your local river, lake or sea
- Strathpuffer 24-hour mountain bike race
- Tough Guy race
- Cut-off date for a midwinter Bob Graham Round
- Cold Water Swimming Championships
- Coldest ever temperature in UK: -27°C

FEBRUARY

- Fort William Mountain Festival
- Edinburgh Mountain Film Festival
- The Pilgrim Challenge
- Big Chill Swim, Windermere
- Usually the best month for sleeping in a snow hole

MARCH

- Spring Equinox (why not try sleeping on the same hill for each equinox and solstice this year?)
- Exmoor Ultramarathon
- Wild watercress season starts
- Devizes to Westminster International Canoe Race (Easter weekend – may be in April)
- Clocks go forward (an extra hour until sunset)
- Puffins begin to return to land to nest

APRIL

- Devizes to Westminster International Canoe Race (Easter weekend – may be in March)
- Nettle soup season
- Viking Way Ultra
- Wild mushroom season begins (ONLY if you know what you are doing!)
- Sheffield Adventure Film Festival (ShAFF)
- Swallows start arriving
- Bluebell season begins

MAY

- Wild garlic season
- Isle of Man's 'Race the Sun'
- London 2 Brighton Challenge
- Southwold Pier to Pub Swim
- Keswick Mountain Festival
- Two Bank Holiday weekends

PUTTING YOUR MIND
AT EASE

The Countryside and Rights of Way Act (The Crow Act), the Right to Roam, Open Access land... these are all important issues for people interested in the legal ramifications of exploring our countryside. Search online for these issues if you feel you would like to know more. But although the specific laws on land access are complicated, the reality of how to behave in the countryside is simple: follow footpaths as much as possible, don't cause any damage to land nor nuisance to people. And be courteous, pragmatic, polite and discreet. Stick to this and you will be absolutely fine.

Despite the enchanting simplicity of just tossing out your bivvy bag onto some unsullied hilltop as the sun sets, there are a few mental hurdles that most first-time 'bivvyers' find themselves having to overcome when sleeping 'wild' as opposed to sleeping in a formal campsite.

• Sleeping in a bivvy bag as opposed to a tent.
• The legality and safety of sleeping wild.
• The practicalities of how to sleep out in a bivvy bag.
• Worries about sleeping wild, particularly for females or people sleeping out alone.

All of this is much easier than you might imagine, and once you have tried it you'll realise how simple it is. Here are a few pointers to try to set your mind at ease.

→ Even after all the nights I have slept wild, I still feel more exposed and vulnerable in a bivvy bag than in a tent. It's a normal way to feel and it adds to the child-like sense of excitement, though the imaginings of ghosts and giant snakes never entirely go away!

→ I recommend doing your first microadventure with a friend or two. You will feel much bolder and less likely to chicken out.

→ You are far safer than you might feel. The reality is that you are more inconspicuous without a tent (though perhaps not to ghosts and vampires...). And sleeping in a bivvy bag on a hilltop is also amusing, which counts for a lot!

→ Although ghosts are unlikely, farmers and early morning dog-walkers are common, but not many of them are likely to stumble across you in your slumbers between dusk and dawn. And if they do, they are overwhelmingly more likely to be amused or curious than angry or threatening. However, just to be on the safe side, I generally try to sleep where I can't be seen. This may mean hopping over a stile away from a footpath, retreating a few metres into a wood or heading to the far end of the beach.

→ If you are particularly nervous (perhaps it's your first time or you are in quite a built-up place) then try this trick. Find a nice spot to sleep in, then move away from it – to a cafe or comfy clump of trees – and relax until nightfall. Once it is dark you can return to the spot you scouted out. Leave again at first light. With this method you can sleep, safely, just about anywhere in the world.

→ Wild camping is legal in Scotland, but not theoretically so in the rest of the UK. Some of England (Dartmoor and the Lake District, for example) is becoming more open to the idea of it. But throughout the UK (and all over the world) nobody has ever complained, told me off, arrested me, or been in the slightest bit concerned on the very rare occasions that I have been 'caught' sleeping wild.

→ There are two answers regarding where you can sleep wild in England and Wales: the technical, legal one is 'almost nowhere (without permission)' and the practical one is 'almost anywhere'. In the same way that nobody would mind you having an afternoon snooze on the beach, nobody minds wild camping, so long as you're not blatantly on private land, near someone's home without asking, or otherwise being annoying.

→ Common sense and courtesy are king, as always. Use your discretion to decide whether your camp spot is appropriate. There's a big difference between sticking a tent up in the middle of a corn field right next to a farmhouse and lighting a massive fire versus discreetly tucking your bivvy bag behind a hedge a few miles away from a village and heading on your way nice and early in the morning.

Overall, sleeping in a bivvy bag for the first time is certainly a slightly unnerving experience, particularly if you are not in a very wild place. But it is also incredibly simple, cheap, fun, memorable and liberating. You just need to try it once or twice to reassure yourself.

HOW TO FIND A PRECISE SPOT TO SLEEP FOR THE NIGHT

Once you have worked out roughly where you are going for your first 5-to-9 microadventure, you might need a few tips to help you find the perfect wild camping spot. Things to look for on your map to identify a delightful sleeping spot include lots of contour lines (a hill) with a flat bit at the top, green areas of woodland, blue areas of water, or even walls to shelter behind in areas of fields away from homes. Look for a footpath leading off the road into quieter areas. Stroll down a path like that for half a mile or so and you're virtually guaranteed to find a nice place to lay your head.

On the map I have ringed some good-looking spots close to a rural railway station to give you an idea of how simple this is. I have never been to this place but I'd be pretty confident that all of these spots would make adequate beds for the night. Remember: almost nobody will want to bother you, even if they knew where you were, which they don't. And, because you are arriving late, leaving early, leaving absolutely no trace and being very courteous and polite, you are not going to be bothering anyone else.

The satellite picture opposite is the same area as the map below it. Although it is difficult to find precise sleeping spots on this view, it is very helpful for one great reason: it reassures me that it will be phenomenally easy to find somewhere secluded and pretty to sleep in this area. I won't cause any problems. Nobody will bother me. So long as I have a little daylight to follow my nose to somewhere that appeals, I know that this will be easy.

But if you do happen to end up arriving in the dark then the process is actually even easier. The dark is the microadventurer's friend, because once darkness has fallen you can just stroll out of the town, fish and chips in hand, and kip in the first peaceful spot you find. Nobody can see you, and you are troubling nobody. Sleep well, enjoy the sunrise, then leave. It's as easy as that.

'The dark is the microadventurer's friend, because once darkness has fallen you can just stroll out of the town, fish and chips in hand, and kip in the first peaceful spot you find.'

Like so many things in life, the anticipation of camping wild is far more difficult than the reality of it. I did it on the majority of days on my four-year ride round the world. For year after year I set off every morning, often in countries that others would label as 'dangerous', with no idea where I would sleep that night. For the first few days it worried me. Gradually I became accustomed to it, and then I began to enjoy a sense of liberation almost impossible to find in normal modern life. I loved my wild camping life, but the only real way that I can convince you that the joys massively outweigh the worries is by encouraging you to give wild camping a go. Once you have tried it a couple of times you will get over your nerves and relish the satisfaction of finding a good spot.

Don't fret too much. Just go. If the night is bright with stars and the grass beneath you is soft then you'll have an exciting, memorable first 5-to-9 microadventure, wherever you are.

In the morning, when you take the train back to work, everyone in your office will think you are mad, but they'll be impressed and jealous too! Post your pictures online with the #microadventure hashtag and make everyone else jealous too.

THE ART OF
SLEEPING WILD

There is an art to finding idyllic places to sleep. Getting out into the wild helps, but there is a little more to it than that. Once you've cracked it then the world opens up.

I feel confident, almost everywhere on Earth, that I am never too far from a quiet field and a sunset all to myself. This has saved me money: if I'm due to be somewhere first thing in the morning, I am as likely to spend the night sleeping on a river bank as spending £50 on a bland hotel chain. I once gave a talk at a posh black-tie event in a seaside hotel. Walking to the hotel from the station I spotted a quiet patch of grass beside the sea. After my talk, I slipped out into the night to sleep under the stars and enjoy a sunrise swim. It was far more memorable than just another night in a hotel room. (An aside: microadventures get you thinking differently about the cost of adventure too. For the price of even the cheapest hotel I could cycle from coast to coast or take a weekend microadventure to France.)

Sleeping wild has saved me from madness too, escaping for a simple blast of fresh air and a change of scene when the real world threatens to crush me for one reason or another.

Wild camping changes the way you observe the world. When I am in a car these days I often catch myself thinking, 'that would be a great spot to sleep the night' as I drive by. It also increases your freedom of movement for it helps take your adventures into more remote places than when you are tied to formal camping grounds. When I cycled a lap of the Isle of Wight (see pages 146–51) I met a fellow cyclist who was envious that I was going to get 'all the way' to the south coast of the island. He had to return that evening to his campsite whereas I was free to push on for as long as I wished.

However, if you are new to wild camping then it can sound daunting to head out to a place you have never been and just hope to find somewhere safe and comfortable to sleep. But it honestly is neither scary nor particularly hard, once you get the hang of it.

For your first wild camping experience, I recommend going with a friend. You will probably feel nervous the first time you sleep in a bivvy on a hilltop. Even sensible adults find themselves worrying about axe-murderers, despite being miles from the nearest human

on a hilltop, consider dropping a few metres down the downwind side of the hill. If you're sleeping on a beach, do it above the high-tide mark (the highest line of washed-up sticks and seaweed). If you don't do this, you are an idiot. None of this is hard: common sense, a little kit and a bit of get-up-and-go is all you need to bag yourself the best morning view you have ever had.

'In our imagination we tend to think that every hedgerow, every copse of trees is patrolled by angry farmers, policemen, and axe-murderers. This is nonsense.'

You can find safe, snug wild camping spots surprisingly close to towns and villages. Follow a footpath just a short distance away from a road then nip behind a hedge or a clump of trees. Nobody has seen you. Nobody will pass this way. Nobody knows where you are. You are safe. I have slept in many ludicrously built-up areas, from a building site in central Malaga to the hard shoulder of a motorway on the outskirts of Dubai. In our imagination we tend to think that every hedgerow, every copse of trees is patrolled by angry farmers, policemen, and axe-murderers. This is nonsense. Think how rarely you see any of those things during daylight. At night they are even rarer. Like everyone (except you and me), they like to sleep in their beds at night, lulled to sleep by terrible television. So don't worry! Use your common sense, be courteous and ask permission if there is anyone to ask permission from. But don't over-think it. You'll feel very open, conspicuous and slightly silly as you lie down to sleep on top of a hill, but you'll soon relax and enjoy the novelty of being right out in nature.

and even further from the nearest axe shop. Grown men catch themselves jumping at the sound of a broken twig, so take a friend with you. You can encourage and rationalise with each other, and together you will realise that a lonely hilltop, beautiful and deserted by day, does not become a gathering point for ghosts and vampires after nightfall. You are far safer on an empty hill than in a town.

Finding a spot to wild camp is about compromise: will you choose the shelter of an old barn or the lee of a cliff in case it rains? Or will you gamble on the full canopy of stars out in the open? It will be glorious if the weather holds but horrid if it doesn't. Getting out of the wind will keep you much warmer, so if you're bivvying

5-TO-9 MICROADVENTURE KIT LIST

The point of microadventures is that you do not need much time, money or specialised equipment to begin with.

Here are the essential bits of kit that you will need for your first 5-to-9 night away, and then some extra items that you might like to buy as your budget and enthusiasm swells. Longer microadventures will probably need more specific equipment, as well as a first aid kit and possibly some repair tools. However, this section only offers suggestions for a quick 5-to-9 microadventure.

Please don't be put off and think you cannot afford a microadventure. You will probably find that you already own most of the things on the basic kit list. If you need any materials for modifying, improving or repairing outdoor gear, then visit the Pennine Outdoor website. You might be able to borrow some bits from a friend, and those things you do have to invest in can be bought cheaply or second-hand. Besides,

eBay will probably be overflowing with unwanted outdoor gear from people who read this book, bought lots of kit, then got rained on or eaten by midges and vowed never to repeat the stupid idea ever again!

BASIC KIT LIST

1. Rucksack – as a rough guide, a 30-litre pack is probably big enough for your first venture. Line it with a bin bag to keep all your gear waterproof.
2. Sleeping bag – don't buy anything special. If you worry that your sleeping bag might not keep you warm enough then just pack as many extra jumpers as necessary. (See page 207 for more advice on sleeping bags.)
3. Orange survival bag – to use as a bivvy bag

to protect you from wet weather. Buy these online or at any camping shop for a few pounds and put your sleeping bag inside. (See pages 204–6 for how to use a bivvy bag.)

4. Foam sleeping mat – essential for getting a half-decent sleep. Put it outside your sleeping bag and inside the orange survival bag. (See page 205 for more information.)

5. Torch (make sure you check the batteries).

6. Rain coat (even in summer).

7. Woolly hat (even in summer).

8. Warm clothes for night time (use a spare jumper as your pillow).

9. Food that doesn't need cooking. Or eat before you go. Have breakfast when you get back home.

10. Water – 2 litres should be plenty.

11. Toothbrush with toothpaste already applied and wrapped in cling film. Use it in the morning.

12. Matches to light a campfire, if appropriate. (See page 221 for fire advice.)

13. Loo roll – although you may want to follow your mum's old advice and 'go' before you set off. (See page 243 for toilet techniques.)

14. Notebook and pen – even if you never write a diary this is a really good chance to jot down a few observations, thoughts and resolutions.

15. Camera – for smug self-portraits and the beautiful sunrise (remember to tag it with #microadventure). Wrap it in a plastic bag in case of torrential non-stop rain misery.

Tell someone where you are going and when you will be back, then go!

NEXT STEP UP:
TAKE ALL THE ABOVE PLUS...

- Camping stove and lighter. (See page 217 for advice on stoves.)
- Swiss Army knife or Leatherman multi-tool.
- Pan – take one that you already have at home, unless you are cooking on an open fire, which destroys pans.
- Simple food such as instant noodles or pasta and tuna or pesto. Tea and coffee. Porridge.
- Cup.
- Spoon.
- Proper bivvy bag (instead of the sweaty orange survival bag).
- A tarpaulin to shelter you in case of rain. (See page 211 for how to build a 'basha'.)

LUXURY ADDITIONS:
TAKE ALL THE ABOVE PLUS...

- A whole tube of toothpaste.
- Inflatable sleeping mat instead of foam mat.
- Moka Pot espresso maker.
- Pillow or inflatable pillow.
- Pyjamas/change of clothes.
- A beer or two, a screw-top bottle of wine or a hip-flask of whisky. Or all of the above.
- Clean pants (they can double as an extra hat if it gets cold. Just remember to remove them before returning to civilisation in the morning).
- Ingredients for a fabulous al fresco meal. (See pages 222–3 for campfire cooking tips.)

THE ANTI-KIT LIST

As important as knowing what to take on adventures Is learning what you do *not* need to burden yourself with.

- Do not take things that you 'might' need – that is for mums to do on family outings. Instead, follow the wise advice from the wonderful microadventure book, *Three Men in a Boat*: 'We must not think of the things we could do with, but only of the things that we can't do without.'
- Expensive, specialist outdoor clothing and equipment. Mallory and Irvine set off up Everest decked out in tweed and woolly jumpers. Okay, so it didn't turn out great for them, but I hope you get my point.
- Expensive, specialist dehydrated camping meals. Captain Scott set off for the South Pole with rations that included biscuits and chocolates. Okay, so it didn't turn out great for him, but I hope you get my point.
- Excessive amounts of spare clothes. Sure, carry enough so as to be warm and comfortable, but if you're in Swindon not Siberia then you probably don't need a 60-litre pack full of kit in midsummer. Remember that it's not good to sleep in wet clothes though, so if wet weather threatens make sure you have enough spare dry clothes to keep you warm at night. If the weather is mild you can just remove your wet layers at night rather than taking a spare set. Putting the wet clothes back on in the morning is horrible, but the discomfort only lasts for a few minutes.
- How many spare clothes you take depends on your personal hygiene levels as well as what you need to go and do the next day. I've often had to carry a suit with me if I am giving a lecture the next day. But if I am just heading back home then I won't even bother taking clean socks or underwear. Don't tell my mum!

- Fancy photography gear is lovely to have on a microadventure, but don't make the mistake of thinking that you can only take good photos with a fancy camera. Most mobile phones these days can capture quality images and video. All the photos from my Tour de Yorkshire (see pages 70–5) were shot on my phone. The important thing is being in the right place and being creative. That will always trump an SLR owner sitting indoors in front of the TV.
- Don't take masses of make-up and toiletries. You've just slept on a hill. You're not going to look your best. Mascara ain't gonna fix that, sir! Wear a woolly hat and dark glasses until you get to a shower if you can't handle it.
- Survival gear to make it through a theoretical apocalypse is not necessary. So long as you've remembered a can opener / bottle opener / corkscrew, you've probably got enough Ray Mears stuff. In other words, a penknife, a lighter and a spoon is usually all you need.

The aim of a microadventure is not to replicate your home on a hilltop. The aim is to pare things away, to simplify, minimise, distil and get to the essence. By all means enjoy yourself, but do so whilst maintaining some sense of simplification. After all, the reduced sauce tastes the richest.

This list is not exhaustive. Its function is only to make you question the gear you put in your bag. For each item you pack, ask these two simple questions:

1. Will I die / fail if I leave this behind?
2. Will I enjoy myself considerably less if I leave this behind?

If you don't answer 'yes' to one of them, then leave it behind.

THE GLORIOUS BIVVY BAG

If you buy only one bit of kit to improve your microadventures, let it be a bivvy bag. They are glorious!

Granted, if it pours with rain you won't have the nicest night of your life in a bivvy bag, but you'll have a story to amuse people with, and that's always worth a bit. Bivvy bags are an essential ingredient to most microadventures. They fit perfectly with the ethos of microadventure. That is, they are simple, cheap, low-hassle, and a little bit silly.

Think of a bivvy as a raincoat for your sleeping bag. It's a thin, waterproof bag that slips over the top of your sleeping bag, enabling you to enjoy a dry night's sleep outside without needing a tent. Like all outdoor kit, bivvy bags range in price and quality.

Here are some advantages of a bivvy bag over a tent:

- A bivvy bag is cheaper than a tent.
- A bivvy bag is a lot smaller than a tent.
- A bivvy bag is easier to pack, carry, dry out and store than a tent: perfect for low-hassle microadventures.
- A bivvy bag is very discreet and enables you to sleep on tiny patches of flat ground.
- In a bivvy bag you are not cocooned from the environment as you are in a tent. When inside a tent, you are basically in a rubbish version of indoors. If you want to be sheltered from

the outdoors, hidden from the sky and the world, then you might as well stay at home rather than swapping your nice house for a cramped, damp, flappy, lumpy version of home. In a bivvy bag you really are outside. You feel the breeze on your face, look up at the stars and sit up to a brilliant view in the morning.

A night in a bivvy bag feels more exciting and more wild than in a tent. Though this, I suppose, might depend on what goes on inside your tent. Not much can go on in a bivvy bag.

There are a couple of disadvantages to the bivvy bag. If it rains you will have a less pleasant night than if you were in a tent / five-star hotel. It is only fair to emphasise this point because when the wind is howling and the rain is trickling down your neck, a night in a bivvy bag is an undeniably rubbish experience. If wet weather is likely then you would be wise to consider a basha (page 211), a tent, or even a night in front of the telly back home. However, as this book is designed to bring out the latent fool within us all, I'll continue singing the praises of a bivvy bag. The exhilaration of those warm dry nights beneath the stars is worth the occasional miserable one. Lastly, even the best bivvy bags leave some condensation on your sleeping bag. For a single-night trip this is no real problem, but for extended use you need to be able to hang your sleeping bag up to dry most days.

Choosing which bivvy bag to buy is not easy. The cheapest way to stay dry is with an orange survival bag. They are a handy thing to own anyway if you are heading into the hills. The chief disadvantage of these non-breathable bags is that you will realise in the morning how much vapour your body gives off in a night! Your sleeping bag will be quite damp. But for a single night microadventure they are absolutely fine. And they only cost a few pounds.

If you are interested in a better quality bag then you need to consider factors such as weight, breathability, 'waterproofability' and cost. Searching online for 'which bivvy bag should I buy' will help you find specific brands and new models. The British Army's bivvy bags are really good; they are made from Gore-Tex®, come in a discreet green colour and are enormous (which is both a good and a bad point). I also used Alpkit, Rab, Mountain Warehouse and Mountain Equipment bivvy bags on the microadventures in this book – they all vary quite a lot in price. Hooped bivvy bags are also an option, especially in midge season, though they do begin to veer towards being a tiny one-person tent. Finally, you can also buy two-person bivvies which open up microadventures to a whole new world of possibilities…

Hopefully I have persuaded you to get hold of a bivvy bag, and if so, here are a few tips on how best to use it.

The bivvy bag goes on the outside of your sleeping bag. I have actually been asked this before! If you are organised it is best to do this before leaving home rather than doing it later in the dark and pouring rain.

Pull the bivvy bag all the way up over your head and pull the draw cord as tight as you wish, then manoeuvre your head into the hood of your sleeping bag. It requires a bit of wiggling and fidgeting, but try to leave a small gap to the open air to breathe out of in order to minimise the build-up of condensation. You'll soon get over the sense of claustrophobia!

I tend to leave my sleeping mat outside the bivvy bag, but if the weather is foul, if you roll around a lot when you sleep or if you have a large bivvy bag then you can put the sleeping mat inside the bivvy bag if you prefer.

Take a large waterproof bag, such as a bin bag, to put all your other stuff into at night, including your rucksack. I tend to use my boots and rucksack as a pillow, though more intelligent people will probably come up with more comfortable solutions.

A night in a bivvy bag is colder than in a tent so make sure you take enough warm clothes. Whatever the season, I always take a woolly hat. Even in summer it's good to pull it down over your eyes so that you don't wake at the first crack of dawn.

To pack up in the morning, simply stuff the sleeping bag and bivvy bag into your rucksack. Make sure you start with the 'foot end' of the bivvy bag otherwise you end up with a massive inflated balloon that won't fit into your pack.

Once you get home make sure you hang up both the sleeping bag and the bivvy bag to dry thoroughly before storing them.

So long as you get half-decent weather for your first microadventure, I am confident that you will agree that a bivvy bag is one of the best microadventure Investments you can make.

SLEEPING BAGS

Choosing a sleeping bag is one of the hardest kit dilemmas. In a dream gear world you would probably own:

➜ A tiny 1-season down bag for ultra-light summer use (or perhaps even a down jacket and a silk sleeping bag liner).
➜ A 2-season down bag for more relaxed summer use.
➜ A 2-season synthetic bag for damper summer use.
➜ A 3-season bag.
➜ A vastly expensive 4-season down bag for those very occasional, but truly cold nights.

Clearly this is not practical for most people, so choosing a sleeping bag becomes all about compromise. Generally speaking, as price increases, so does the bag's warmth, and so does the warmth to weight ratio. The other thing that greatly affects the price of a sleeping bag is whether it is filled with down or synthetic material. Down is warmer, lighter and more expensive. It also performs terribly in wet conditions, when a synthetic bag is a much better option.

I generally opt for a light bag combined with wearing more clothes. It is important to make one piece of kit serve multiple purposes. A down jacket is good to wear in camp as well as for sleeping in, whereas a heavy sleeping bag only helps when you are sleeping. However, almost nothing is worse than those long awful nights when you're wearing every scrap of clothing you've got, you're in your sleeping bag, you've done press-ups galore and you're still bloody cold and torturing yourself through the long, long hours until dawn with thoughts of that big fluffy sleeping bag you left at home to save a bit of weight...

If you are just looking for a sleeping bag for a microadventure rather than a long expedition, I would recommend using whatever you already have and taking along as many supplementary clothes as necessary rather than buying anything new. There is no point spending loads of money for the sake of a bit of extra warmth or weight-saving if you are not going to use the bag very often. Seriously, any old sleeping bag, plus a woolly hat and a few jumpers will be fine.

If you decide that you do want to buy a new sleeping bag, you need to answer these key questions to help you narrow down your choice:

1. What will the temperature normally be like when you use the bag?
2. What is the coldest temperature you will ever face? (In other words, how much protection do you need to ensure that you won't die?) As a general rule, a bit of misery is fine, death a little less so.
3. Will you be mostly dry (get a down bag) or mostly wet (get a synthetic bag)?
4. How much money do you want to spend?

Out on the frozen Arctic Ocean a couple of years ago I used a pile liner with a massive four-season synthetic bag. Rowing across the Atlantic Ocean, I used a sleeping bag from Tesco. In other words, the right sleeping bag for the job depends very much on what you are going to use it for.

KEEPING YOUR GEAR
DRY IN ALL WEATHERS

Even in summertime it's worth taking precautions to keep your gear dry. Nothing can ruin a trip like a wet sleeping bag after a sudden downpour or falling whilst crossing a river (amusing though it may be to your friends). So using waterproof bags inside a rucksack is a good habit to get into. Not only does it help keep things dry, it also makes packing and unpacking simpler. For example, I have one bag that contains my sleeping gear, another with camera kit, and so on.

Whether you are rafting, swimming or just out and about, nothing protects your kit better than a roll-top dry bag. They are available in a range of sizes and degrees of durability and waterproofness. If you are using the dry bag inside a rucksack then durability is not a big issue, but if the bag is likely to get battered by rocks, branches and brambles, you will need a sturdy model.

Using a dry bag correctly is crucial but simple. Put all your stuff inside, trying if you can to have something soft at the top to aid the seal (such as a jacket or sleeping bag). Carefully roll down the top several times then clip the straps together. Be careful when purchasing your dry bag to be clear exactly how waterproof it claims to be. If in doubt, use two, one inside the other. For quick overnight trips or an impromptu swim to an island, a bin bag will work fine in place of a dry bag. Twist the top of the bag round and round to ensure it is completely closed. If you trap air inside the bag before closing it then it will float well whilst you swim.

SHELTER FROM THE STORM

I love bivvy bags and believe they are integral to the spirit of this book, but they really are not much fun when it is pouring with rain. Character building, perhaps. Fun? No. So if there is a threat of rain you might consider expanding your microadventure kit list (see pages 198–202) to include a 'basha'.

A basha is army slang for a simple shelter made from a tarpaulin. Rig it properly above your bivvy bag and you'll get good, uninterrupted sleep even in snow or heavy rain. A single dry night makes it well worth the small cost, the couple of hundred extra grams and the tiny hassle of assembly.

(If, however, you are eager to spend loads of money, then specialist tarpaulin shelters such as the MLD Trailstar or GoLite Shangri-La – opposite – are fantastic.)

HERE'S WHAT YOU NEED TO BUILD YOUR BASHA:

Tarpaulin with eyelets Get it from a pound shop, hardware shop or online. The colour and size are up to you, but 2.5 x 3m (8 x 10ft) would be a pretty luxurious size to begin with, and suitable for up to two people.

Bungees You'll need at least two, but having up to six would increase the pitching options.
Tent pegs You'll need at least two, but up to six would increase the pitching options. Alternatively, you can just use sticks.
String Optional, but it helps increase your pitching options.

You can rig up a basha however you like, according to what is available to hang it from. All you are trying to do is create a roof above the spot where you will sleep. Fences, trees, walls and even bicycles can be used. You just need to find a flat piece of ground to lie on and a couple of points to attach the tarpaulin to above that spot. Bear in mind that if it rains really hard then water will begin to run across the ground. Make sure you are not lying in a prospective stream or pond! Ensure that falling rain or snow will run down off the tarpaulin rather than forming a large and potentially disastrous puddle above your head.

And if the weather is ridiculously foul, don't forget the old saying that any fool can be miserable! B&Bs, retreating home, or simply postponing the microadventure for another time are all options... I won't consider you a wimp. Much.

CREEPY CRAWLIES

One of the common arguments I hear about not wanting to sleep in a bivvy is because of creepy crawlies in the night! This, like worries about axe-murderers and poltergeists, is something that requires a little bit of non-hysterical, rational thinking to overcome. Britain is not Australia. We have woodlice and worms, not box jellyfish and black widows. Even our only poisonous snake, the adder, is so timid that you will only encounter one if you try very hard.

However, the one exception to Britain's generally benign wildlife is the lowly midge. Do not underestimate a midge. Tiny they may be, but midges can turn even the most sangfroid of souls into a thrashing, raging beast. Prevalent in many rural areas in the summertime, particularly in the North, midges can ruin a pleasant evening outdoors.

There are a couple of precautions you can take to help minimise midge misery. Midges are attracted to dark clothing, so dress in light colours. They are also more active on warm, still mornings and evenings, so try to be either moving or indoors at those times. A midge net (covering your head or your entire body) is a useful accessory, as is midge repellent. More than one rugged Scotsman has recommended Avon's Skin So Soft body lotion as being quite effective...

A tent is certainly preferable to a bivvy bag during the worst midge times of year. However, the only really effective solution is to camp in a high and breezy spot. You can also search online for a helpful midge forecast.

Whilst a midge can ruin your evening, they do no long-term damage. Ticks, on the other hand, will not spoil your day but can lead to bigger problems. It is important to be aware of ticks when roaming around the countryside.

The NHS website explains: Lyme disease is a bacterial infection spread to humans by infected ticks. Ticks are tiny arachnids found in woodland areas that feed on the blood of mammals, including humans. Tick bites often go unnoticed and the tick can remain feeding for several days before dropping off. The longer the tick is in place, the higher the risk of it passing on the infection. Lyme disease can affect your skin, joints, heart and nervous system.

Parts of the UK known to have a high population of ticks include:

- Exmoor
- The New Forest
- The South Downs
- Parts of Wiltshire and Berkshire
- Thetford Forest, Norfolk
- The Lake District
- The Yorkshire Moors
- The Scottish Highlands

The best way of preventing Lyme disease is to avoid being bitten when you are in wooded or heath areas known to have a high tick population. The following precautions will help:

- Wear a long-sleeved shirt.
- Tuck your trousers into your socks.
- Use insect repellent.
- Check yourself, your children and pets for ticks.
- If you do find a tick on your skin, remove it by gently gripping it as close to the skin as possible, preferably using fine-toothed tweezers, and pull steadily away from the skin. Never use a lit cigarette end, a match head or essential oils to force the tick out.

SOME ADVICE
ON BICYCLES

Choosing a bicycle is not easy. There are many variables to consider, so my main advice is to do as much cycling as you can, both day rides and overnight microadventures, before you buy a new bike.

This will help you get a feel for the type of cycling you enjoy, how much you really enjoy it, and how much money you wish to spend.

I suggest you begin on any bike you can get hold of. A mountain bike, road bike, shopping bike or folding bike are all absolutely fine for a 5-to-9 overnight adventure. You could even cycle round the world on any of those bikes. So don't let the quality of bike stop you getting out there. The more you ride, the more you will come to understand your needs.

Panniers are the best way for carrying your kit on a cycling adventure, but you'll have to fit racks to your bike (on the back and perhaps on the front too), as well as getting hold of some panniers. Some bikes cannot take racks, in which case you can clamp a rack to your seatpost. These cannot carry very heavy loads but are suitable for short overnight trips (for example, the Tour de Yorkshire on pages 70–5). An old-fashioned saddle bag can carry much the same amount of gear too.

The option that requires the least planning and specific cycling gear is to just wear a rucksack. I did that for most of the cycling chapters in this book. You need to be a little careful to make sure you can still see traffic over your shoulder and that the extra weight does not make you too wobbly. And you will definitely get a very sweaty back and an even-more-sore-than-usual bottom!

If, after all this, you decide that you do love cycling enough to merit buying a decent bike, then go to your local bike shop and start asking them lots of questions. The hardest thing is to be clear in your own mind about exactly what you want the bike to be mostly used for. Also search online to investigate whether you are able to save money from the government's cycle to work scheme.

BIKE BITS TO TAKE ON A MICROADVENTURE

- Helmet – you're not legally required to wear one in the UK, but it's probably a good idea. Doubles as a blackberry-collecting vessel.
- Lights – in case you have to ride after dark.
- Pump – doubles as a device for warding off attacks from dogs in Macedonia.
- Spare inner tube, puncture repair kit and tyre levers.
- Bicycle multi-tool – like a Swiss Army knife for bikes.
- If you are going further than a little overnight trip it's worth carrying a few cable ties and some gaffer tape (wrap a length around on itself rather than taking the whole roll).

THE MOBILE MICROADVENTURE KITCHEN

A camping stove is a really useful bit of kit to buy once you feel that you enjoy microadventures enough to use it regularly. Here is a brief explanation of some of the different types available.

Gas stove

These are cheap and simple to use (see left). You simply screw the attachment into a gas canister, open the valve and light it with a match or a lighter. It then works exactly like a gas hob in your kitchen. Gas canisters are available at all camping shops in the UK and come in a range of sizes depending on the length of your trip. It's my stove of choice for a simple little trip, but I'd never take one on a large overseas expedition due to having to find specialist camping shops to buy replacement fuel. A Jetboil is a souped-up version of a gas stove, excellent for alpinism or rowing oceans.

Trangia stove

A simple, effective and nostalgic alcohol-burning stove. The downside is that it is bulky, fiddly and pretty slow at cooking.

Vargo Titanium Hex Stove

A stove that will appeal to both the Lightweight gear community and Bushcraft types too, even if a carefully-positioned trio of stones achieves more or less the same job as this fold-out titanium twig-burning stove. It is very eco-friendly too, compared to using disposable gas canisters.

MSR

If you are planning a long trip or a remote expedition then the MSR range of stoves are probably for you. They are expensive to buy but an excellent investment. They burn with virtually any sort of fuel, making it perfect for travel in regions where you might not find a camping shop.

Kelly Kettle

These water boilers are pleasingly retro and very efficient. You can boil water extremely quickly with just a handful of twigs. This is a good stove for young families as it's (relatively) safe and simple for kids to begin learning their camping skills with.

Beer can stove

An invention of genius. A thing of beauty. Indispensable to the lightweight fanatics. Easy to make. Satisfying to show off to your friends. Surprisingly efficient. Beer must be drunk prior to construction. A wonderful thing! Burns with pure alcohol (surgical spirit) from the chemist.

How to make your beer can stove

- ➲ Drink a can of beer.
- ➲ Cut the top off the can.
- ➲ Cut the bottom five centimetres off the can.
- ➲ Cut the top section of the can so that it's one centimetre longer than the bottom part.
- ➲ Crimp all the way around the top of the can. These are the little gaps the combusted fuel will burn up through.
- ➲ Insert the top half of the can into the bottom part.
- ➲ Make a tiny hole in the top half of the can. This allows air into the stove as the fuel burns. It's ready to go!

You can watch a video of it being made here: www.alastairhumphreys.com/how-to-turn-a-beer-can-into-the-only-camping-stove-youll-ever-need

Potjie or Dutch Oven

These cast-iron cooking pots come in a range of sizes from a single person pot up to vast cauldrons. They are expensive, totally impractical and wonderful. If you enjoy cooking outdoors then stick one on your Christmas list to Santa. You'll enjoy it for your whole life.

Pan

As well as a stove you'll also need a pan to cook stuff in. When you start out there is no point in buying anything other than a very cheap, basic 'mess tin' for a few quid.

As you find yourself using it more and more, you might wish to progress up to a lightweight titanium pot costing lots and weighing not a lot. Or you may not. My main recommendation is to buy a pan larger than you suspect you might need. Lightweight obsessives might shudder at this, but I would gently suggest that at least 99% of the gram-counting, titanium pan-toting men (it's always men) would be as well to do 10 extra press-ups a day to compensate for the extra 20g of pan and extra 20kg of spare tyre...

Cutlery

I set off to cycle round the world with a spoon 'borrowed' from my university canteen. If you are heading out for a night away you can therefore either take a normal spoon like me, or you can buy an elaborate 'spork' (a spoon, knife, fork combination) or a super lightweight expensive titanium spoon. You might have sensed by now where I lie on the saving weight obsession in the outdoor community. However, when entering races where weight really is at a premium I use a plastic child's spoon (and also a child's toothbrush).

For simple trips the only utensils I carry are a multi-tool and a spoon. Once you go all out for an enormous potjie you might as well take a ladle, a PVC chopping board and even a decent kitchen knife too.

A foil windshield is a useful accessory for all stoves; it protects the flame and minimises heat loss to reduce cooking times. I always take two lighters, a flint and steel or a spare box of matches.

Multi-tool

A multi-tool such as a Leatherman or Swiss Army knife is a useful thing to take on all microadventures. They come in a staggering range of shapes and sizes. You'll have to decide for yourself which tools you actually need (a knife), and which ones you just like playing with or showing off to your friends...

Coffee

If the idea of enjoying a decent cup of coffee in the morning appeals, then make a little extra space in your pack for a Moka Pot espresso maker. They come in a range of sizes.

If filter coffee is more your thing then consider an insulated coffee press mug. If travelling light is more important to you, opt instead for a sachet of instant coffee and a folding mug.

WILD DRINKING

No, not that sort of wild drinking ... finding drinking water in the wild. I may be a little on the reckless side here (so search online for more scientific and expert advice) because I drink water straight from streams all over the UK and have never suffered any consequences. If you are more cautious and sensible than me then you might want to consider purifying your water, particularly as you get further away from the river's source. Options for purifying water include boiling it or purifying it. I have used iodine drops on all my travels through about 90 countries over the past 18 years and I am still alive, but it has recently been banned by the EU as a water-purifier! The other method for purifying water is filtration. You can buy water filters from camping shops and online retailers. I have never used one but I am sure they are both marvellous and essential.

ADVICE ON HAVING A FIRE

Having a campfire to sit round and tell tall tales whilst you toast marshmallows makes any microadventure more magical. But, perhaps more than for anything else in this book, the rules of common sense and courtesy apply about where it is appropriate to have a fire.

→ Do not light a fire where there is a risk of it spreading – peat moors, corn fields, dry forests and petrol station forecourts are all pretty obvious examples. Whenever you light a fire you must be certain that you will be able to extinguish it at any time. Never light a fire on private land without permission where it could cause offence or be an eyesore. As a general rule, only light fires in places where nobody is likely to come by until all trace of it has grown out. Always keep your fire small.

→ If possible, dig a hole before lighting a fire. This will help keep it out of the wind and contain the fire. Replacing the earth and turf in the morning (once the fire is absolutely extinguished) also helps prevent ugly scorch marks and minimises the visual impact of the fire. If you cannot dig a hole then ring your fireplace with large stones to keep it contained. Never use soft, hollow or wet rocks as they could explode. If the ground is particularly wet (or on snow) lay a base of green logs to keep the fire off the wet ground until it is established.

→ A fire requires three things to burn well: heat, fuel and oxygen. Without any of these the fire will fail. Remembering this will help you figure out what is going wrong if you are struggling to get your fire lit.

→ Begin with a small pile of tinder (dry grass, leaves or paper). Build a pyramid of kindling on top of it (very thin dry twigs). Make sure you have more kindling close to hand, as well as larger sticks a couple of centimetres in diameter and a few larger branches. It's vital that all the wood you use at first is dry; once the fire is roaring you can get away with damper stuff. The best is dead wood found hanging in trees rather than lying on the ground where it can absorb moisture. Once you have gathered and assembled your wood it is time to light the fire. Like all heroic outdoor folk I can light a fire without matches. I use a lighter.

→ Ignite the tinder. As the kindling on top of it begins to catch light, blow gently on the flames. Blow steadily with a pursed mouth, like blowing through a straw, for the best effect. As the fire takes hold you can blow harder. Gradually add bigger sticks to the fire. Once you are confident that the fire is established, add larger branches. If you want to cook on the fire you need to create a good bed of embers from these larger branches before you begin, so get them burning as early as you can.

DOCUMENTING AND SHARING YOUR MICROADVENTURE

The best reason to go on a microadventure is because you want to. There might be nothing more to it than that. Do the trip, come home, don't tell a soul. But many people enjoy documenting their experiences too, and some then like to share those stories.

You can document an adventure in many different ways. I once met a lady who climbed Kilimanjaro carrying an easel, paints and a mop because she enjoyed painting with a mop. So there is hope for the occasional box of watercolours making it up into the Quantocks. I really hope so.

As wonderful as paints, pencils and paper may be, these days most people record their lives digitally. Whilst I hope that people mostly use their time in the hills to distance themselves from phone calls and emails, I also love the smartphone's power for pithy, concise storytelling.

Advocating such-and-such a social media site in a paper book is a fool's game, outdated the moment it hits the shelves (though I firmly believe that 'Facebook' and 'Twitter' will never take off...). So all I want to do is encourage you to give some thought to what you want to document and how you want to do it. And, most importantly, to establish *why* you want to do it. Once you are clear in your mind about those things it will help you choose whether you want to take photos, capture video, record audio or write down your story. Done thoughtfully I feel this can really add to your experiences.

My only word of caution is this: please, please remember to enjoy the actual experience. Trade Tweets for birdsong. Take time away from your camera to sit still for a while and really look, to listen to the silence, to feel the winter air nip your nose and ears, and to spend quality time either with yourself (cheesy, but important) or with your fellow microadventurers (fun and important).

IMPROVING YOUR MICROADVENTURE PHOTOGRAPHY

1. Take a camera with you. And don't just take a camera: actually take it out of your bag and begin using it! This sounds obvious, but it makes all the difference. Even if it's just the

3. If you have a DSLR camera then learn how to use the different modes. You're on a spectacular hilltop. It's getting dark but there is a lovely late, soft light. Your bivvy bag and rucksack lie heroically in the foreground. You decide to take a photo. It will be a great shot. *FLASH* goes the camera, on automatic mode. The result? A pitch-black background and some dazzles from the reflective bits on your bags. The simple solution for a decent exposure? Just open the aperture or slow the shutter speed. Even my phone now has an app for shooting at slower shutter speeds.

'Whilst I hope that people mostly use their time in the hills to distance themselves from phone calls and emails, I also love the smartphone's power for pithy, concise storytelling.'

4. If you are shooting on your phone then don't rely on Instagram's filters to post-produce your picture and make you and your mates look hip (or as hip as sitting in the rain in an orange plastic bag eating a Scotch egg can ever be). There are scores of apps – some free, some paid – that can do a much better job of polishing your pics, such as Snapseed, which I often use before posting my pictures on Instagram.

5. Don't just take a photo from the position you happen to be standing in. You have to move to get the ideal viewpoint. Step closer or further away. Crouch down. Lie down. Climb a tree. Experiment.

6. Start to learn about photography composition techniques such as the rule of thirds, leading lines, filling the frame, focal points, active space and framing.

camera on your phone, get into the habit of taking regular photos, whatever the weather. The times when you really can't be bothered to take photos are probably the times you should be shooting.

2. Although you probably are using a digital camera, try to imagine that it is a film camera. In other words, think that every picture you take will cost you 50p. This should help you make a little more effort with your photography. Pause, think, compose, and only then press the shutter. It amazes me how often I see people taking photographs whilst actually still walking, like Arnold Schwarzenegger shooting from the hip on the move.

TREES WORTH HUGGING

Ten of Britain's most iconic trees: do you recognise them all?

1. Ash
2. Beech
3. Elm
4. Oak
5. Hornbeam

6. Silver birch
7. White willow
8. Horse chestnut
9. Scots pine
10. Hawthorn

LEARNING BIRDSONG

An easy way of reminding yourself that we still live in a wild world (even a garden can be a pocket of wildness) is by learning the calls of some wild birds.

Your garden visitors are not tamed; they arrive from thousands of miles away, use your garden for a while and then leave again when it suits them. They are above planning regulations and green belts and disputes over garden-fence boundaries. They are wild. They come, go, live, fight, mate and die amongst the delineated patchworks of our regimented lives and gardens.

I am not very good at recognising birdsong, but I am finding it really rewarding as I begin to learn more. Birdsong is not something that works very well in writing, so search online for the excellent RSPB guide to listen to different bird calls (www.rspb.org.uk/wildlife/birdguide/name). There are also several apps that do a similar thing on your smartphone.

If you're not sure where to start, try these birds. They are either common in your garden or in the countryside, or else their calls are so distinctive that they are easy to learn. It's a good starting point.

- Blackbird
- Robin
- Magpie
- Green woodpecker
- Curlew
- Swallow
- Skylark
- Grouse
- Buzzard
- Rook
- Pheasant

CLOUD SPOTTING

Not only is a little bit of knowledge about clouds handy for forecasting the weather, it also increases your enjoyment of the outdoors

Whether it is recognising birdsong, picking out stars, or knowing that Cirrostratus clouds suggest you'll not get rained on tonight, the more knowledge you have about different aspects of the natural world you are immersed in, the more satisfying your microadventures will be.

It is easy to do a quite accurate short-term weather forecast by identifying the clouds you can see in the sky from the diagram opposite:

Stratus
Often signals imminent light rain.

Cumulus
Scattered ones suggest fine weather.

Cumulonimbus
These impressive, enormous anvil-shaped clouds often foreshadow heavy storms.

Cirrostratus
If these begin to cover the sky, rain may be on the way within the next 24 hours.

Cirrus
These extremely high clouds are seen when the weather is fine. Watch their movement to know which direction a weather front is likely to arrive from.

Cirrocumulus
'Mackerel sky, storm is nigh' goes the old saying. But not always...

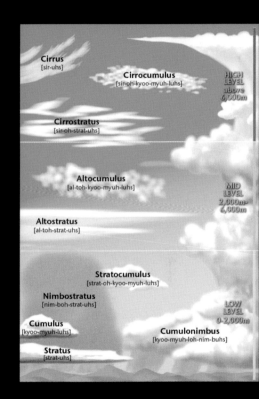

Cirrus
[sir-uhs]

Cirrocumulus
[sir-oh-kyoo-myuh-luhs]

HIGH LEVEL above 6,000m

Cirrostratus
[sir-oh-strat-uhs]

Altocumulus
[al-toh-kyoo-myuh-luhs]

MID LEVEL 2,000m–6,000m

Altostratus
[al-toh-strat-uhs]

Stratocumulus
[strat-oh-kyoo-myuh-luhs]

Nimbostratus
[nim-boh-strat-uhs]

LOW LEVEL 0–2,000m

Cumulus
[kyoo-myuh-luhs]

Cumulonimbus
[kyoo-myuh-loh-nim-buhs]

Stratus
[strat-uhs]

STAR GAZING

It would be a cold-hearted soul who gazed up at the stars on their first night in a bivvy bag and was not struck with a measure of awe.

I love watching the moon's steady march across the sky, and picking out planet Venus or the tracks of satellites and the pale smudge of the Milky Way as my eyes grow accustomed to the dark.

Your enjoyment of the skies will increase if you are also able to identify a few of the most prominent constellations of stars. The following are some of the easiest for northern hemisphere microadventurers to spot at various times of the year:

CASSIOPEIA

Cassiopeia, named after a beautiful but vain queen in Greek mythology, is one of the easiest constellations to locate. It looks like a large 'W' (or, at times, an 'M').

PLOUGH

Not only is this satisfyingly easy to spot, the Plough (also known as the Big Dipper or Great Bear) makes finding the North Star, Polaris, extremely simple.

The Plough looks a little like a saucepan. To find Polaris, simply extend the line of the 'front' of the saucepan and about two 'pan lengths' away you will see another bright star. This is Polaris. As Polaris is positioned, more or less, above the North Pole, it is a useful way to orientate yourself north.

POLARIS

PLEIADES

It's hard to give a simple instruction as to how to find Pleiades, also known as the Seven Sisters. I have chosen it because it is a bright, compact star cluster which often catches my eye at night. My extremely crude method is this: find Polaris in the manner described opposite. Once you hit Polaris, 'turn right' until you see a small, bright cloud of stars. Once you have seen it a few times it will start to grab your attention more often.

ORION

Orion or, more precisely, Orion's Belt is perhaps the best-known trio of stars. It is particularly easy to spot on winter evenings. You need to look for three bright stars, close together, and in a neat straight line. Once you've spotted it you should also notice Sirius, the brightest star in the sky.

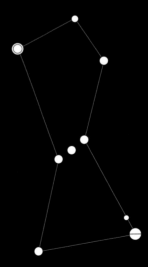

REDUCING THE COST OF YOUR TRAIN JOURNEY

Travelling by train in Britain can be an expensive and soul-destroying experience, but here are a few basic tips to save yourself some money on your microadventure.

1. Buy your tickets up to 12 weeks in advance using websites like The Trainline, Megatrain or Red Spotted Hanky. You can save significant amounts of cash this way. Always try to travel during off-peak times.

2. It is a brave soul who tries to take a bicycle on many of Britain's intercity trains. I am lucky to have a folding bike which gets round the exemptions, otherwise I try to travel by foot on any microadventures that involve an intercity train. You certainly can take bikes on trains, they just often require pre-booking onto a specific train. Check with your train operator for their policy (http://goo.gl/fBPmRZ). Annoyingly, generally you cannot book your bike at the same time as buying tickets online, though you can on the East Coast Trains' site.

3. Book an exact-train-only ticket on your outward leg if you know precisely when you want to travel, with an Open Off-Peak return option for coming home. This saves you some money but still gives your plans a bit of flexibility too.

4. Two single tickets can sometimes be cheaper than a return ticket.

5. Experiment with split-ticketing. Buying a ticket from, say, London to Penzance can often cost much more than buying a series of tickets for different stages of that journey. It requires a bit of fiddling and experimenting online, but the savings can be large, particularly if only part of your journey takes place during peak hours.

6. The sleeper train between London and Scotland is one of Britain's best adventures and can be very reasonably priced. You get a night's accommodation, a train to a far-off place, and the magical feeling of going to sleep in smelly Euston station and waking up in the Scottish Highlands. If you take the sleeper train, do a bit of a mental cost-benefit analysis before plumping for the cheap seats rather than a bed. I once had to take the night train to the most important exam of my life. I chose the cheap seats and didn't sleep a wink. I somehow passed the exam, but never again will I plump for the cheap seats! The Seat61 website has masses of information about this train.

7. To save even more money, consider travelling by intercity bus. A word of warning: some of those epically slow bus journeys of my youth rival the worst mountain-top-rainstorm-no-food-bivvies... But they certainly are cheap.

WHEN THINGS
GO WRONG

My aim with this book is to remove the barriers to entry that can sometimes make the world of adventure seem elitist. I wanted to make it easier for 'normal people' (by which I mean 'not adventurers' – the speech marks highlighting the awkwardness of these categories) to get out and experience the countryside and wilderness. I hope this book gives people the tools and the confidence to cycle for hundreds of miles, to skinny dip on New Year's morning, and to sleep under the stars.

But there is a risk in all of this, because mountains and rivers can be dangerous places. So I repeatedly urge common sense throughout this book. Before heading into remote places, especially by yourself, please make sure you do these things:

◆ Tell people where you are going and when you will be back.

◆ Make sure you are properly equipped for the conditions, and for a potential worst-case deterioration of the conditions. On high ground this is likely to include carrying an orange survival bag, a whistle (and knowing the rescue signal: six long blasts, pause for a minute, repeat), a charged phone, a torch, warm clothes and emergency rations. You must aim for total self-reliance except in case of a serious accident.

◆ Set up your mobile phone to be able to contact the Emergency Services via SMS (for when signal is weak or if you are unable to speak). To register for this send the word 'register' in a text message to 999. You'll get a message back which you must then reply to with 'yes'. Do this right now, before you ever need it!

◆ Check the weather forecast before you go.

◆ Be aware that Mountain Rescue teams and the RNLI are volunteers. Being an idiot can put other people's lives at risk. Take responsibility for your own actions and learn more about staying safe in the hills at the appropriately named www.safeinthehills.org.uk website or from Mountain Rescue (www.mountain.rescue.org.uk/mountain-advice).

◆ Wild places are absolutely capable of exposing your weaknesses – in skill, in equipment, in fortitude, in judgement. They can be fierce and merciless. This is both their appeal and their threat. Whilst challenging yourself is part of the lure of wild places, be sure to remain on the right side of the line that separates sensible, calculated risk-taking from recklessness. It is an invisible and ever-changing line, however, so be very cautious.

◆ Make sure you are experienced enough to judge potential hazards in the environment you are in, and are able to safely remove yourself from that environment if necessary. If in doubt, start with something easier. Take a course at somewhere like Plas y Brenin, Glenmore or Mountain Training to build your competency in outdoor disciplines.

◆ If you do require emergency assistance, call 999 and ask for the police or the coastguard. The police will arrange assistance from Mountain Rescue if they need it. You must give them your grid reference or GPS coordinates (your smartphone can provide this information if it has reception), so ensure that you know how to find this information in advance of ever needing it.

FIRST AID

If you are heading out into the wild you ought to be familiar with some basic first aid techniques. Methodology and best practice are continually evolving so search online for up-to-date information and local organisations you can train with. Remote Emergency Care and Wilderness Medical Training are both great places to start.

Topics you should be familiar with include:

- Putting together and using a first aid kit
- Anaphylactic reactions
- Burns
- CPR
- Choking
- Cuts, open wounds and blood loss
- Head and spinal injuries
- Hypothermia and hyperthermia
- Safe movement of injured casualties
- Shock
- Sprains, fractures, dislocations and breaks

THE MICROADVENTURE CODE OF CONDUCT

Enjoying adventurous activities in the countryside is a good thing. We have a right to get out there and do fun things in the world's wild places. But enjoying microadventures also carries a few responsibilities. I suggest we all need to:

- Care for and champion our dwindling pockets of countryside.
- Ask permission, be gracious and courteous.

- Arrive late. Depart early. Leave no trace.
- Share the countryside generously with other people who are working or engaged in leisure activities in the same spaces.
- Be responsible for our own actions and safety.

More learned bodies than me have made efforts to lay down guidelines for appropriate behaviour in the outdoors. Some of the initial rules of the Country Code, dating back to the 1930s, make a pretty good starting point:

- Enjoy the countryside and respect its life and work.
- Guard against all risk of fire.
- Keep your dogs under close control.
- Keep to public paths across farmland.
- Use gates and stiles to cross fences, hedges and walls.
- Leave livestock, crops and machinery alone.
- Take your litter home.
- Help to keep all water clean.
- Protect wildlife, plants and trees.
- Take special care on country roads.
- Make no unnecessary noise.

Simple, also, is The Scottish Outdoor Access Code:

- Take responsibility for your own actions.
- Respect people's privacy and peace of mind.
- Help farmers, landowners and others to work safely and effectively.
- Care for the environment.
- Take extra care if you are organising a group, an event or running a business.

Be safe. Be courteous and sensible. Have fun. That should suffice.

LEAVE NO TRACE

This is simple. Leave no trace. Take all your litter with you. 'Litter' means everything you brought with you. This absolutely includes banana skins and orange peel, for they are an eyesore that can take a couple of years to decompose.

Go even further than removing all your litter: take home other litter that you find and help return the countryside to being as clean as it ought to be. Leave the countryside cleaner than you found it.

Caution: The next paragraphs contain the word 'poo'. No sniggering, please.

Going to the toilet is slightly more complicated than litter. For a 5-to-9 overnight microadventure you can probably avoid poo-ing in the wild. As your mum used to say, 'You should have gone before you set off'.

But if you do need to go, I'd encourage you to dig a hole, about six inches deep, then bury your poo and loo roll far from footpaths or water sources. Burning your loo roll (unless you are in a fire risk area) is also a good idea. If you are very dedicated you could take it home with you as the paper takes far longer to break down than the poo. Fill in the hole and cover it well with soil or leaf litter.

Poo does actually decompose faster if it's left in open air, but please only do this if you can be sure that nobody will be passing by for weeks to come.

And a plea for dog owners: please, please get your dog to poo away from footpaths. Or bag the poo and take it home with you. Above all else, don't bag your dog poo then leave it hanging on a tree or fence like some sort of grotesque Christmas tree decoration. Seriously – who does this? Stop it!

HEALTH, SAFETY AND RESPONSIBILITY

The activities described in this book have risks and can be dangerous, and many of the sites featured are in remote locations. Please be prepared before embarking on any microadventures. The author and publishers have gone to great lengths to ensure the accuracy of the information herein, but they cannot be held legally or financially responsible for any accident, injury, loss or inconvenience sustained as a result of the information or advice contained in this book. Swimming, jumping, diving, cycling, walking, sleeping outdoors or any other activities at any of these locations is entirely at your own risk.

ADDITIONAL RESOURCES

This book only scratches the surface of so many different things. These resources may help you delve a little deeper into whatever specifically interests you. Where I have not offered a specific web address (because they tend to come and go over time) I have just listed phrases that should lead you to useful sites if you type them into a search engine. Hopefully this will help you search more quickly and effectively. I have tried to offer resources for everything I mention in the body of the book. Where things are relevant for more than one chapter I have only included them in the section for the earliest chapter.

① THE 'ONE DAY' ADVENTURE
P. 18

- The Crowsflight app encourages purposeful meandering by pointing you in the direction of your final destination. The decisions on how to get there are up to you. The first few times you use it are free.
- My books about cycling round the world are called *Moods of Future Joys*, *Thunder and Sunshine* and *The Boy Who Biked the World*.
- Search online for a list of Britain's 50 Greatest Trees.
- Search online for a list of Protected Views in London.
- Organised long-distance cycling challenges: London to Brighton Bike Ride, Dunwich Dynamo, Lord of the Lochs Sportive, Exmouth Exodus, Hell of the Ashdown, Skylark Sportive in Yorkshire, Birmingham to Oxford or an Audax event.
- Geocaching.com.

② UNDER A HARVEST MOON
P. 22

- Search for a Lunar Calendar that tells you the time of moonrise and the dates of full moons. You can also find information about sunrise and sunset times.
- Point your smartphone at the sky and the Star Walk app identifies the stars you are looking at. It's magical!

③ WALKING HOME FOR CHRISTMAS
P. 25

- Twitter and Instagram are both a great way of sharing your microadventures and also seeing what other people are up to via the #microadventure hashtag. You can follow me or say hello via @al_humphreys.

④ USE YOUR WEEKEND
P. 28

- Search online for a list of Mountain Bike Centres in the UK. I went to Afan Forest Park Mountain Bike Centre.
- Search online for the British Coasteering Federation.
- Search online for the Trailwalker and Trailtrekker Charity Challenges.

⑤ STEP OUT OF YOUR FRONT DOOR
P. 30

- Dark Sky areas.
- RSPB Bird Song.
- Download the Bleep Test MP3.

7 A COMMUTER'S ADVENTURE
P. 36

➔ Martin, my 'real' commuter, wrote this about his experiences: www.martinblack.com/2013/04/wild-camp-in-a-hertfordshire-wood.
➔ An example of how walking every street in your town can grow from a microadventure to a huge adventure: www.imjustwalkin.com.

8 A JOURNEY AROUND YOUR HOME
P. 40

➔ You can get a map that shows your own home right in the centre of it. They look great on the wall and make a really nice present: www.ordnancesurvey.co.uk/shop/custom-made-maps.html.
➔ Xavier de Maistre journeying around his room: goo.gl/PjniVd.
➔ OS MapFinder app works well for both iPhone and Android.

9 CATCH IT, COOK IT, EAT IT
P. 45

➔ Search online for information about the Environment Agency's fishing permits.

10 ENTER A RACE
P. 48

➔ The Strathpuffer 24 hour mountain bike race.
➔ See page 51 for a list of other races to try as well as www.findarace.com and www.ultramarathonrunning.com/races/uk.html.

12 A GLASGOW NIGHT OUT
P. 54

➔ Explore the Campsie Fells.
➔ See page 185 for ideas of wild places within easy reach of Britain's big cities.
➔ Listen to Chris exploring the Scottish outdoors every Saturday on BBC Radio Scotland: @BBCOutofDoors.

13 COAST TO COAST – AN ANCIENT JOURNEY
P. 59

➔ Sustrans National Cycle Network.
➔ Mountain Bothies Association.
➔ World Heritage Sites in UK.
➔ Map for Hadrian's Wall cycle route: www.sustrans.org.uk/ncn/map/route/route-72.
➔ Dress like a serious explorer: TX Maxx: www.tkmaxx.com.
➔ Visit Hadrian's Wall.

14 COAST TO COAST – A WILD JOURNEY
P. 66

➔ Information about the overnight sleeper train between London and Scotland: www.seat61.com.
➔ Information about packrafts and different-priced alternatives: www.alastairhumphreys.com/packraft-info.
➔ English White Water: The British Canoe Union Guidebook.
➔ Packrafting! An Introduction and How-To Guide, Roman Dial.
➔ BoardFree: The Story of an Incredible Skateboard Journey across Australia, Dave Cornthwaite.
➔ Bicycle Dreams – a film by Stephen Auerbach about the Race Across America.
➔ Mountain Bike Coast to Coast information: www.c2c-guide.co.uk.
➔ The Dragon's Back Race across Wales.
➔ The TGO Challenge.

15 A CREDIT CARD ADVENTURE
P. 70

➔ Tour de Yorkshire website and route: www.letourdeyorkshire.com.
➔ The Golden Journey to Samarkand by James Elroy Flecker.
➔ Visit Masham's breweries.
➔ Learn more about the Bob Graham Round in

Richard Askwith's excellent book *Feet in the Clouds*.

 WOODS AND FORESTS
P. 77

➡ Find a forest near to you through the Forestry Commission website or The Woodland Trust.

RIVER SWIM
P. 80

➡ www.wildswim.com.
➡ See the books on page 247 for a few suggestions about wild swimming books.

ROMAN ROAMIN'
P. 84

➡ Ordnance Survey's Roman Britain Historical Map and Guide.

CLOSE YOUR EYES. GO!
P. 100

➡ Torridon Cafe, Torridon, Achnasheen, Ross Shire, IV22 2EZ.
➡ Torridon is the setting for one of Britain's greatest triathlon races, The Celtman: www.cxtri.com.

FAMILY TREE
P. 106

➡ *Lost Lanes* by Jack Thurston is an excellent book for anyone interested in cycling microadventures in South East England. Jack is currently working on a series of books about other lost lanes.

CANAL JOURNEY
P. 111

➡ Devizes to Westminster International Canoe Race takes place every Easter weekend. Entries open 1 January on www.dwrace.org.uk.

➡ Ordnance Survey Inland Waterways Map of Great Britain.
➡ Search for Canoe Canal Permit to find up-to-date information about the permits required to paddle on canals.

WILDERNESS ADVENTURE
P. 118

➡ You can get to Knoydart by ferry (search for Knoydart ferry online) or on foot (look on the Knoydart Foundation's website for information). Accommodation in Inverie ranges from posh down to a municipal campsite to sleeping wild on the hills. For anything but the latter option you should book in advance. The Old Forge Inn and The Pottery Cafe serve food and there is a small shop, though it only stocks absolute basics.
➡ The night train from London goes to Fort William, where you can change for the scenic train to Mallaig and the short ferry to Inverie.

BUILDING A WILD HUT
P. 124

➡ Kevin's ongoing Wild Hut project is documented here: www.100wildhuts. blogspot.co.uk.

A JOURNEY ON THE TUBE
P. 127

➡ If you plan to do a journey on inner tubes like this you will need a paddle. It need not be special – the paddle for a rubber dinghy will suffice. Tow gear behind you in a dry bag, or consider getting an extra inner tube just for carrying the kit.
➡ Anyone aspiring towards a shed of their own will enjoy the Shedworking blog and book and my favourite website of www.cabinporn.com.

32 FROM SUMMIT TO SEA
P. 139

- Search online for the highest point in all the counties.
- *Walking the County High Points of England*, David Bathurst.

34 A CIRCULAR JOURNEY
P. 146

- Red Funnel Ferries travel daily to the Isle of Wight.

35 A RAFTING ADVENTURE
P. 153

- Millican Dalton's cave is on the eastern flank of Castle Crag, Borrowdale. If you visit please leave no trace behind, and take out some of the mess that other people have left there.
- *Kon-Tiki: Across the Pacific by Raft*, Thor Heyerdahl.
- *The Happiest Man in the World: An Account of the Life of Poppa Neutrino*, Alec Wilkinson.
- *The Adventures Of Huckleberry Finn*, Mark Twain.

37 A JOURNEY TO THE END OF MY COUNTRY
P. 167

- The Northlink ferry from Aberdeen to Lerwick runs seven days a week.
- *On The Rocks: A Lightkeeper's Tale*, Lawrence Tulloch.

38 AN M25 ADVENTURE
P. 176

- *London Orbital*, Iain Sinclair.
- *M25: Travelling Clockwise*, Roy Phippen.

BOOK SUGGESTIONS TO GIVE YOU IDEAS FOR A MICROADVENTURE OF YOUR OWN

- *The 39 Steps*, John Buchan
- *As I Walked Out One Midsummer Morning*, Laurie Lee (the first part of it, in England)
- *Winnie-the-Pooh*, A. A. Milne
- *Swallows and Amazons*, Arthur Ransome
- *Three Men in a Boat*, Jerome K. Jerome
- *Rural Rides*, William Cobbett
- *Lost Lanes*, Jack Thurston
- *In Pursuit of Spring*, Edward Thomas
- *The Book of the Bivvy*, Ronald Turnbull
- *Running High*, Hugh Symonds
- *Feet in the Clouds*, Richard Askwith
- *Waterlog*, Roger Deakin
- *Walking Home*, Simon Armitage
- *The Gentle Art of Tramping*, Stephen Graham
- *Mountain Days and Bothy Nights*, Dave Brown and Ian R. Mitchell
- *To the River*, Olivia Laing
- *The Wild Places*, Robert Macfarlane
- *Millican Dalton: A Search for Romance and Freedom*, Matthew David Entwistle
- *Extreme Sleeps: Adventures of a Wild Camper*, Phoebe Smith
- *Britain and Ireland's Best Wild Places: 500 Essential Journeys*, Christopher Somerville
- *Wild Swimming: 300 Hidden Dips in the Rivers, Lakes and Waterfalls of Britain*, Daniel Start
- *Wild Swim*, Kate Rew and Dominick Tyler
- *Food for Free*, Richard Mabey
- *The Natural Navigator*, Tristan Gooley
- *How to Shit in the Woods: An Environmentally Sound Approach to a Lost Art*, Kathleen Meyer

WANT HELP HEADING OUT ON YOUR MICROADVENTURE?

I hope that this book has inspired you to get out and try a microadventure for yourself. No matter how busy you are, how big a city you live in, or how unfit you are, you can still get out into the wild, watch the sunset and sleep under the stars. This book is just a start. I hope it is the spark that starts a fire.

If you are looking for more information and encouragement then please get in touch with me on Facebook, Twitter or through my website. I'll try my best to help or encourage you. You can also sign up for my free occasional newsletter at www.alastairhumphreys.com/subscribe.

If you think that your business could benefit from the space, time and perspective of a night away from the city on a beautiful hilltop, get in touch too. I'll make it happen – alastair@alastairhumphreys.com.

If you do go on a microadventure, please share your stories and photos online. Tag them #microadventure so that everyone can find them. I'll do my best to share and promote the best ones. If you have enjoyed and benefited from microadventures, the best thing you can do is pass the idea on to other people who might feel they want to give it a go.

 Zap the code to go directly to my website (www.alastair humphreys.com) and sign up for my monthly newsletter.

INDEX

A

Aberdeen 168
adventure, definition of 14
Afan Forest Park 29, 244
Aonach Eagach Ridge 165
Areas of Outstanding Natural
    Beauty (AONBs) 184
Audax event 21, 244
Autumn Equinox 23, 138, 143, 188

B

Back to Basics 96–9
'basha' (shelter) 74, 178, 202,
    205, 211
Bath 86
BCU handbook to English
    White Water 110
Beacon Hill 140
Bealach na Bà 157
Ben More, Scotland 34
Ben Nevis 87, 143, 184
Berkeley Plane (Britain's most
    expensive tree) 24
bicycles:
    popularity of cycling 70
    rail company policy 193, 240
    some advice 214–15
    see also mountain bike and
        under individual
        microadventure name
'Big Five safari challenge' 24
birchbark canoe 126
bird spotting 24
birdsong, learning 236
Birmingham to Alvechurch canal
    113

bivvy bag 5, 33, 37, 40, 52, 53, 56,
    61, 70, 71, 72, 73, 75, 101,
    104, 105, 109, 121, 137, 149,
    176, 178, 199, 202, 211, 233,
    247
    advice on staying warm in
        winter 117
    art of sleeping wild and 196, 197
    creepy crawlies and 212–13
blue whale, Natural History
    Museum 24
Bivvy Challenge 144–5
Bluemull Sound 174
Bob Graham Round 75, 245–6
bothies 54, 61–4, 245
breakfast outdoors 31
Brecon Beacons 165, 184, 185
Britain:
    landscape, man's effect
        upon 16
    wild 184–5
British Canoe Union 110
Brompton bicycle 167
Brue, River 86
Building a Wild Hut 124–6, 246
butterflies 24
Buttermere Triathlon 51
Buttertubs Pass 73

C

Cadair Idris, Gwynedd, Wales 34
Cairngorms 67, 184
calendar of the microadventure
    year 186–8
Caldey Island 105
Caledonian Canal 113

camera 22, 40, 74, 155, 199, 203,
    210, 232–3
Camley Street Nature Reserve 184
camping:
    shop 199, 217–19
    stove 31, 68, 117, 140, 202, 217
    wild 50, 56, 58, 69, 80, 105,
        156, 175, 181, 190–1, 195–7
Canal Journey 111–13, 246
Canvey Island 116
Cape Wrath, Scottish Highlands
    122
Catch it, Cook it, Eat it 45–7, 245
Cateran Trail, Scotland 87
cathedral or sports stadium, cycle
    to biggest in your county 21
Circular Journey 146–51, 247
Cleveland Way 65
climbing hills:
    in the dark 32
    in the mist 102
Close Your Eyes. Go! 100–3, 246
cloud spotting 237
Coast to Coast – A Wild Journey
    66–9, 245
Coast to Coast – An Ancient
    Journey 59–65, 245
coast to coast journeys,
    alternative 69
coasteering 29, 244
code of conduct 242
Coed Y Brenin Enduro 51, 189
Coledale Horseshoe, Lake
    District 165
commute:
    cycle a different route 24

shake up your 27
walk or run the route of your 36
Commuter's Adventure 36–9, 245
compass:
　bearing, travel along a 103
　using a 20, 81, 103, 109, 226
cooking, campfire 222–5
Cornwall 69, 93, 107, 137, 150
Corrachadh Mòr 143
Cotswold Way 65
Craig y Fan Odu, Brecon Beacons 165
Credit Card Adventure 70–5, 245–6
Crib Goch, Snowdonia 165
Crossing England 69
Crowsflight app 20, 244
CTC 63, 69
Cuillin Ridge 157, 158, 162
Culra bothy, Scotland 64
Cumbria 122, 140, 153
cutlery 218–19
Cwm Dulyn bothy, Wales 64

D
Dark Sky areas 31, 244
Dart 10K 51
Dart, River 51, 83, 110
Dartmoor 65, 110, 184, 191
de Maistre, Xavier 40, 245
Deakin, Roger: *Waterlog* 81, 247
deer spotting in Greenwich or Richmond Park 24
Defoe, Daniel 87
Derwent, River 154, 155
Devizes to Westminster canoe race 111, 113, 186, 246
Devon 51, 69, 83, 85, 99, 130
Dickens, Charles: *Great Expectations* 117–18
dinner in the garden 31

disused railway lines converted into walking or cycling paths 64
Ditchling Beacon, East Sussex 34
documenting and sharing your microadventure 232–3
Dragon's Back Race 69, 245
dream big, start small 58
drinking, wild 219
Dungeness 79
Dunnet Head 143
Dunwich Dynamo 21, 51, 188, 244
Dwyfor, River 83

E
East Cowes 151
East Lancs Road, from Old Trafford to Anfield, run down the 107
Enter a Race 48–51, 245
Erme, River 83, 110
Esk, River 110
Essex 105, 176, 181
Etive, Scottish Highlands 83
Euston Road, London 167
excuse-busting 199
exercise in the park instead of the gym 31
Exeter Cathedral 84
Exmouth Exodus 21, 244

F
5-to-9 Adventure 32–5
　how to find a location for 192–3
　kit list 198–203
Facebook 17, 189, 230, 232, 248
Fairy Pools, Skye 83
Family Tree 106–7, 246
field to sleep in, in search of 38
Fiennes, Celia: *The Journeys of Celia Fiennes* 87
fire advice 220–1

first aid 242
Flow Country 34
Forest of Dean 79
Fosse Way 84, 86, 87
Fred Whitton Challenge 65
friend's house, cycle to 21
From Summit to Sea 139–43, 247
Fuchs, Vivian 149

G
gadgets 230
Gars-bheinn 163
geocaching 21, 103, 244
Glasgow Night Out 54–8, 245
Glencoe's Woodland 79
Gloucestershire 87
Glyndwr's Way 65
Going Out for Dinner 132–6
GPS 21, 227, 241
Grand Union Canal Race 51
grandparents, ride to the birthplaces of 107
Great Pond, Epsom Common 144
grid reference NH02020 (Britain's most isolated spot) 122
Grwyne Fawr bothy, Wales 64

H
Hadrian's Wall 50, 60–2, 65, 87, 245
hammock, sleeping in a 31
Harewood 71, 74
Harrogate 73
Hatton Lock Flight 113
Haughton Green bothy, Northumberland 64
Hawes 73
health, safety and responsibility 243
Hell of the Ashdown 21, 244
Hertfordshire 176, 180, 245
high points:

climb to your local high point and then visit every prominent high point you can see 43

travel in your lunch hour to the highest point you can see from your office 43

visit the highest three peaks of your county 143

High Speed 2 rail link, follow the route of 107

hills:
climbing 29, 33, 34, 101, 124, 125, 133, 140, 141, 162, 163
sleeping on 33–5, 121, 137, 140–1

Horsey Island 105

Hounslow Heath 24

howies Coed Y Brenin Enduro 51

'Hutchy' hut, Scotland 64

I

Ilchester 86

illusion of wildness can refresh the soul 118

Impromptu Escape From the Office 114–17

Inaccessible Pinnacle 163–4

Instagram 17, 71, 189, 230, 233, 244

Irish Sea 143

Island Camp 104–5

Isle of Man: 'Race the Sun' 51, 186

Isle of Wight 29, 43, 146, 147, 196, 247

J

John Muir Trust 184

John O'Groats 83, 168

Journey Around Your Home 27, 40–3, 245

Journey from Source to Sea 108–10

Journey on the Tube 127–31, 246

Journey to the End of My Country 166–75, 247

junk rafts 155

K

Kearvaig bothy, Scotland 64

Keats, John 87

keeping on time, tips for 35

Kendal Mountain Film Festival 13, 189

Kennet and Avon Canal 111

Kent 25, 27, 99, 117, 176, 178

King Henry's Mound in Richmond Park to St Paul's Cathedral, cycle from 21

kitchen, the mobile microadventure 216–17

Knap of Howar 84

knots 231

Knoydart peninsula 118–21, 246

L

Lake District 143, 154, 165, 184, 185, 191, 213

Lake Windermere 110

Lancashire 106

Land's End to John O'Groats challenge 63

leave no trace 243

Leeds-Liverpool Canal 113

Leicestershire 140

Leven, River 110

Leyburn 73

Liatach, Torridon, Scotland 34

light pollution 23, 31

Liverpool 106–7, 185

Lizard Point 143

Loch Coruisk, Isle of Skye 122, 162

Loch Insh, Cairngorms 68

London to Brighton Bike Ride 21, 186, 244

London Underground 149, 173

London Zoo 24

Long Distance Walker's Association 65

long-distance challenges 65

Lord of the Lochs Sportive 21, 244

Lord's Cricket Ground 168

Lowestoft Ness 143

Lyme disease 213

M

M25 Adventure 176–81, 247

Macfarlane, Robert: *Wild Places* 163–4, 247

Mallaig 118

Malvern Hills 34, 185

mammal spotting 24

Man vs Mountain 51

Maol Bhuidhe bothy, Scotland 64

map, how to orientate 227

marathon route, your local 75

Meanach bothy, Scotland 64

microadventure:
calendar 186–8
code of conduct 242
community aspect 58
definition 14
documenting and sharing 232–3
how to have your own 182–249
why busy people need 114
see also under individual microadventure name

Millican Dalton: A Search for Romance and Freedom (Entwistle) 153–4, 156, 247

Milton Keynes microadventure 53

Monmouthshire and Brecon Canal 113

Monopoly board, cycle all the streets from the 27

moon:
blue 138
harvest 22–4, 138

lunar eclipse 138
Paschal full 113
super- 22, 138
Mountain Adventure 157–65
mountain bike:
    challenge 143
    trail centre 29
    see also under individual race
      name
Mountain Bothies Association
    54, 245
mountaineering 28–9, 102
Muckle Flugga 168, 175
Munro (a mountain higher than
    3,000 feet) 34, 65, 101, 162

N

National Parks 184
National Rail cycle policy 193,
    240
National Scenic Areas, Scotland
    184
National Trails 65
National Trust 184
navigating by the sun 228–9
Neutrino, Poppa 155
New Forest 79, 184, 213
Newcastle 60
Norfolk 139, 184, 213
Norfolk Broads 113, 184
Norfolk Coast Path 65
North Downs 65, 185
North York Moors 184
North, finding using stars 116
Northumberland 62, 64, 87, 184

O

Odyssey, The (Homer) 168, 173
Offa's Dyke 65, 87
Okement, River 110
oldest tree in Scotland, Wales
    or England, make a pilgrimage
    to 21

'One Day' Adventure 18–21, 244
Open Access Land 184, 190
Ordnance Survey map 64, 101,
    227, 246
Osea Island 105
Ottery St Mary 85
Out of Office Experience 52–3
Outdoor Swimming Society 83
Oxford to Cambridge on Boat
    Race weekend, run from 107
Oxford University track,
    Iffley Road 75

P

packrafts 66, 67, 108, 109, 110,
    159, 167, 168, 172, 174, 245
parents' birthplaces, visit your 27
Pauntley to London, travel from
    107
Peak District 51, 184–5
Peddars Way 65
pedestrianism 75
Pembrokeshire 65, 99, 184–5
Pembrokeshire Coast Path 65
Pennine Bridleway 65
Pennine Way 65
Pentland Hills, outside
    Edinburgh 34
Perseid meteor shower 72–3, 188
Perth, Scotland 124, 125
photographs, taking 23, 58, 149,
    203, 232–3, 248
Pilgrim's Way 87
pilgrimage to the home of Banks,
    Cohen, Charlton, Moore,
    Wilson, Stiles, Ball, Peters,
    Hurst and Hunt 107
pizza oven 126
Plym, River 110
Polaris 117
Polldubh Falls, River Nevis,
    Scotland 83
Pontcysyllte Aqueduct 113

pubs:
    Britain's most northerly –
      Hilltop Bar 122, 173
    the remotest pub in mainland
      Britain – the Old Forge Inn
      122
putting your mind at ease 190–1

Q

Quantock Hills, Somerset 87
quitting 122, 165

R

Race Across America 69
Rafting Adventure 152–6, 247
railway stations 20, 24, 110
Ramsay's Round 65
Ramsey Island 105
Rannoch Moor 66
Red Bull Steeplechase 51
reptile spotting 24
resources, additional 244–7
Ridgeway 65
River Swim 80–3
rivers:
    catching fish 45–7
    damaged, diverted or buried 16
    journey from source to sea
      108–10
    river swim 31, 80–3
    using rivers and canals 110
    see also under individual
      microadventure and river
      names
Robertson, James 87
Robin Hood's tree 61
rolling a dice to decide
    your plans 103
Roman Empire 60–3, 84–7
Roman Roamin' 84–7, 246
Royal Geographical Society 13
Royal Society for the Protection
    of Birds (RSPB) 184, 236, 244

Rubha Hunish bothy, Scotland 64
Rum Cuillin traverse, Inner
Hebrides 165

S
Samson Island 105
Sat Nav 20
Scafell Pike 110, 140, 143
Scavaig, River 162
Scilly Isles 105, 143
Scotland 21, 29, 34, 48–51, 52,
54, 55, 66–9, 87, 93, 101,
108–10, 118–26, 158, 174,
184, 191, 213, 240, 242, 245
*see also under individual
place and
microadventure name*
Scotland's Great Trails 65
Scottish Outdoor Access Code 110
Sea Adventure 88–93
sea kayaking 88–93, 159, 162
second-highest three peaks in
Britain 143
'self-transcendence' race 51, 188
Severn, River 108
Severn Estuary 108
Shard, The 37, 38
Shenavell bothy, Scotland 64
Sherwood Forest 79
Shetland Isles 130, 167, 168, 173
Skipper's Island 105
Skipton 71
Skokholm 105
Skomer 105
Skye 93, 122, 157, 162, 164, 184
Skylark Sportive 21, 244
sleeping bags 16, 30, 33, 34, 35, 40,
68, 72, 75, 84, 85, 92, 102, 117,
121, 124, 126, 136, 137, 13, 144,
155, 156, 168, 173, 178, 181, 189,
198, 199, 204–10 *see also*
bivvy bag
sleeping mats 75, 208

sleeping wild 17, 30, 32–3, 38, 107,
190–1, 194–5, 196–7, 209, 246
Sligachan 158
Slow Adventure 92
Snowdon 83, 87, 143, 165, 184–5
Solstice Adventure 137–8
Somerset 85, 87
South Downs 65, 184–5, 213
South West Coast Path 65
South West peninsula 69
Spey, River 66, 67, 68–9
spin a bottle when you reach
a junction 103
Spring Equinox 138, 186
spring tide 91
Spurn Point, East Yorkshire 122
St Albans 36, 37, 38, 39
St Cuthbert's Way 87
star gazing 238–9
Step Out of Your Front Door 30–1,
244
stew, ultimate microadventure
222–3
Stonehenge 107
Strathpuffer 24-hour mountain
bike race 48, 49, 50, 130, 186,
245
Suffolk 51, 184
Suileag bothy, Scotland 64
Suilven, Inverpolly, Scotland 34
Sumburgh Head 168
Summer Solstice 138, 188
sunrise times 35
sunset times 35
supermoon 22, 138
Sustrans National Cycle Network
63, 245
Swaledale 73
Swallows and Amazons (Arthur
Ransome) 36, 104, 247
Swimmer, The 83
swimming, wild 31, 80–3, 143
Symonds Yat Rock 83

T
taster weekend course 29
Tennyson, Alfred Lord 149
TGO Challenge 69, 245
Thames, River 65, 69, 81, 84, 87,
113, 116, 176, 179, 181
Thomas, Edward 87
Thurston, Jack 106, 246
Torridon, Scotland 34, 101, 130,
246
Tour de France 70–1
Tour de Yorkshire 29, 203, 214,
245
Trailtrekker 244
Trailwalker 29, 244
train journeys 20, 24, 39, 193,
240, 244
treehouse 126
trees 21, 24, 50, 61, 234–5, 244
Tryfan, Conwy, Wales 34
tube:
walk a line you're familiar
with 39
Twitter 26, 54–5, 58, 98, 179, 189,
230, 232, 244, 248
Tyne, River 60

U
Under a Harvest Moon 22–4, 244
Unst Island 175
Use Your Weekend 28–9, 244

W
Wade, General 87
waking in the countryside 33, 34,
98, 102, 105
walking:
100 miles in 24 hours 75
every street in your town
or city 39
the route of your commute 36
*see also under individual
microadventure name*

wagers 75
Walking Home for Christmas 25–7, 244
Wasdale, Cumbria 122, 143
Wastwater 141, 143
Watling Street 38
Welsh 3000s 65
West Highland Way Race 51
Weston, Nick 97, 99
Wharfe, River 71, 72, 83
when things go wrong 241
Whittington, Dick 107
wild Britain 184–5
wild camping 190–1
wild hut 124–6, 246
wild places near cities 185
wild swimming 31, 80–3, 143, 246
Wilderness Adventure 118–23, 246
Wildlife Trust 184
Wiltshire 87, 213
Winter Solstice 138, 189
Wistman's Wood 79
Woodland Trust 184, 246
Woods and Forests 76–9, 246
Worcestershire Beacon,
    Malvern Hills 34
World Heritage Sites 61, 245
world-record running pace,
    cycle a marathon in 21
World's Biggest Liar competition
    140
writing shed 126

Y

Yarmouth 149
Yell Sound 173
Yorkshire:
    Dales 70, 71, 72–3, 106,
        155, 184–5
    Three Peaks 65
    Wolds Way 65

ACKNOWLEDGEMENTS

Thank you to all my friends who have accompanied me on the stories in this book. Thank you to everyone in the online #microadventure tribe who has enjoyed, shared and evangelised the idea of microadventures over the last few years.

The following people and companies have all helped either with this book or with the growth of microadventures: Tomo Thompson, Rob Bushby, Joanna Penn, Leon McCarron, Paul Deegan, Tom Allen, Rob Symington, Dom Jackman, Richard Bannister, David Hieatt, howies, Trek Bikes, Osprey Packs, Alpkit and Mountain Equipment.

Thank you to Ben for convincing HarperCollins to take a punt on me, and to Myles Archibald, Julia Koppitz, Kate Tolley, Myfanwy Vernon-Hunt and Steve Boggs for turning my vague ideas about mucking around in the hills into a proper book, and for making me actually sit behind a computer for long enough to write it.

MICRO
ALASTAIR HUMPHREYS
ADVEN
TURES

LOCAL DISCOVERIES FOR GREAT ESCAPES

WILLIAM

William Collins
An imprint of HarperCollins*Publishers*
77-85 Fulham Palace Road
London W6 8JB

WilliamCollinsBooks.com

First published in Great Britain by William Collins in 2014

20 19 18 17 16 15 14
11 10 9 8 7 6 5 4 3 2 1

ISBN 978-0-00-754803-3

Publishing Director: Myles Archibald
Senior Editor: Julia Koppitz
Editor: Kate Tolley
Design and layout: This Side
Production: Chris Wright

Colour reproduction by FMG
Printed and bound in China